THE ABUNDANCE OF OUR FAITH

THE ABUNDANCE OF OUR FAITH

AWARD-WINNING SERMONS ON GIVING
Plus Suggestions for Group Discussion

EDITED BY

TERRY SWEETSER AND SUSAN MILNOR

SKINNER HOUSE BOOKS
BOSTON

Copyright © 2006 by the Unitarian Universalist Association of Congregations. Published by Skinner House Books, an imprint of the Unitarian Universalist Association of Congregations, a liberal religious organization with more than 1,000 congregations in the U.S. and Canada. 25 Beacon Street, Boston, MA 02108-2800.

Printed in the United States

ISBN 1-55896-516-5
978-1-55896-516-4

Cover: The four most recent winners of the Stewardship Sermon Award (from top down)—Cecelia Kingman Miller, Naomi King, Bonnie McClish Dlott, and Patrick T. O'Neill.

Library of Congress Cataloging-in-Publication Data

The abundance of our faith : award-winning sermons on giving, plus suggestions for group discussion / edited by Terry Sweetser and Susan Milnor.
    p. cm.
  ISBN-13: 978-1-55896-516-4 (pbk. : alk. paper)
  ISBN-10: 1-55896-516-5 (pbk. : alk. paper) 1. Christian giving--Sermons. 2. Stewardship, Christian--Sermons. 3. Unitarian Universalist Association—Sermons. 4. Unitarian Universalist churches—Sermons. 5. Unitarian Universalist Association—Doctrines. 6. Unitarian Universalist churches—Doctrines. I. Sweetser, Terry, 1946- II. Milnor, Susan, 1951-

BV772.A28 2006
248'.6—dc22

2006011878

10 9 8 7 6 5 4 3 2 1
08 07 06

We gratefully acknowledge permission to use the following material:
Excerpt from *Maniac Magee* by Jerry Spinelli. Copyright © 1990 by Jerry Spinelli. Reprinted by permission of Little, Brown and Co., Inc.

CONTENTS

INTRODUCTION

AT THE HEART of Unitarian Universalism is the faith that every person can make a meaningful difference in our communities and in the world. We have faith in generosity, a conviction that our shared gifts of love and labor can heal ourselves and others. To be fair, this is a challenging faith. Most of us waver in it and in our generosity, fearing that our open-hearted religion may lead us beyond the bounds of safety, that it might call us to give too much away.

This fear is particularly strong—and difficult to talk about—when it comes to money. We harbor a feeling that it is crass to discuss personal income, rude to ask for money, and indiscreet to even bring up the subject of financial obligation. But talk about it we must. Money is not "the root of all evil" but a symbol of value. Spent one way, it can make us comfortable, boost our self-image, and make us feel secure. Spent another way, money becomes the tool of our faith and our commitment to the things that matter to us. The allocation of our resources is a matter of choices, and talking about it proves both necessary and spiritually healthy.

The sermons in this collection serve as models for talking about fundraising in terms of a theology of money. They shine a light on the fundamentally religious nature of giving, and they do so with graciousness, wisdom, humor, directness, and understanding. Rather than fearing that we will ask for or be asked for too much, these sermons help us appreciate the opportunity that fundraising offers us to look deeply at the things that we value. Giving is a way to express our beliefs and use our financial power in positive ways.

At the nexus of faith and fear, we learn stewardship. From Old English roots meaning "keeper of the hall," *stewardship* is the recognition that our privilege gives us the power to make good happen. The hall we keep is for helping hope, never for protecting privilege. Fundraising in Unitarian Universalist congregations is the work of learning stewardship, and it lies at the core of our theology.

A story from my own days as a young minister, more than thirty years ago, illustrates how we can all learn to think differently about fundraising. When I looked at my first congregational budget, I was confused by something called APF. What could this expensive item be? What would the more than $3,000 be buying for the church, and more importantly, for its ministry?

We needed so much. The old IBM typewriter was on its last legs. The ditto machine needed upgrading to a real mimeograph. We had no music director, the church secretary came in only ten hours a week, and the director of religious education was trying to run a church school of eighty young people on five hours a week. Meanwhile, I wanted enough in the minister's travel budget to get me to our Unitarian Universalist Minister's Association retreat.

A quick conversation with the church treasurer told me that APF meant Annual Program Fund. "What's that?" I asked.

"That," he told me, "is dues. You know, what we pay to Boston to be a member of the Association. It's a head tax." From there I learned that the APF wasn't really about dues or taxes, but about what was called *Fair Share*. It turned out that then, as now, the Fair Share was calculated by the number of members a congregation had. Our district staff person assured me the amount was neither dues nor a tax but rather a gift we were supposed to give to the Unitarian Universalist Association each year.

I was young and green, so you won't be surprised that all this made me mumble under my breath, "What about *our* fair share? What about *my* fair share? What about not sharing at all?" Muttering away, I called our congregational president, a renowned jurist, A. J. Priest, who was also the chair of the Denominational Connections Committee.

A. J. took his call to complete my ministerial training very seriously and realized that my complaints constituted a teachable moment. "Sweetser," he said, "get down to my chambers. Now!" There was a delightful clarity about governance in the early seventies. I went.

In twenty-five minutes, A. J. introduced me to the concept of generosity. "Give," he said, "not until it hurts but until it helps. Remember, your money is really your time transformed by work in the world. The more you do, the more time and money you will have to share. Generosity is about the freedom that comes from sharing and giving."

He went on to say that just as people need liberating by generosity, so too do congregations. Our church, he pointed out, gave its collection once each month to support a good community cause. Doing that was giving until it helped, but it was also freeing the institution from a sense of scarcity.

"Now, Sweetser," he said, "about the Annual Program Fund. Giving our Fair Share is what we need to do for our own sense of abundance and generosity. But we also need to give our Fair Share because we are part of a religion that is larger than this congregation. We own that larger part and we must maintain it.

"By the way," A. J. said, "you need to preach about this. You have to learn to talk about money and sharing and generosity. You need to give your Fair Share of effort to the cause. If you don't, you and our movement will become irrelevant, and our religion will become scarce."

I have preached about the Annual Program Fund. I have even entered the Annual Program Fund Sermon Contest, though I have never won. The sermons in this book did win. They are outstanding because of that, but even more because all of the authors took on their fair share of the effort to keep us from becoming scarce.

If you are a minister, these sermons and the questions that

follow them can provide invaluable inspiration anytime you need to galvanize your congregation to reach its most generous giving potential. Read carefully, and you will identify excerpts that can serve as perfect texts for a stewardship sermon or a Commitment Sunday service.

Ministers or lay leaders seeking to build a board or congregational retreat around stewardship will find great insights and good suggestions here. Select a sermon that seems most pertinent to your congregation's situation and ask participants to read it before your retreat begins. The questions provided at the end of each sermon are intended for discussions in just such congregational settings. The questions also encourage you to make the connections between the general ideas presented and your own congregation's situation.

When leadership in a congregation wants to share its evolving vision of responsible and exciting stewardship with the wider congregation, these sermons can help. Organize a congregation-wide retreat and adapt one of these sermons as a keynote speech to open your event. Small groups can then tackle the discussion questions.

Whether you are a professional or lay leader, the most important aspect of these sermons is that they move the consideration of stewardship from the practical matters of technique into the deeper issues of meaning and theology. Ultimately, a congregation's willingness and ability to take a visionary stance in its stewardship depends on making connections to what its members care about and what lends meaning to their lives. We think these sermons and questions can provide a terrific start.

Terry Sweetser

THE LAND OF ENOUGH

CECELIA KINGMAN MILLER

Pacific Unitarian Universalist Fellowship
Astoria, Oregon

With disarming honesty, Cecelia Kingman Miller admits that she is jealous of the Religious Right. Indeed, she wishes that we liberal religionists were as good at focusing, organizing, and spreading our message as our more orthodox counterparts. She gives voice to the vague feelings of discontent and doubt that many of us grapple with when we contemplate the force of the Religious Right in America over the past several years. What makes Miller's sermon inspirational is its challenge to us to do the same for our religion. She writes, "The thing is, our God—the force of Love in the universe, the unnamable yet ever-present Divine Spirit of Life, the God of trees and rivers and bears, the God of the poor and dispossessed, the God of refugees and hungry children, the God of Thoreau and Emerson, Channing and Parker, Francis David and all the nameless martyrs of our faith—our God deserves glory too." Glory Hallelujah! Preach it!

Ultimately, people will only give to our congregations if they are in touch with their deepest longings and their most daring sense of mission. In fact, embracing these feelings offers the only authentic, lasting reason for our congregations to exist. Being our best means ensuring our survival. So may it be. –S. M.

1

I GET THESE CATALOGS and magazines in the mail; I'm sure you do, too. They are filled with pictures of things I must buy and bodies I will never have, trips I ought to go on, and cars I should drive. We live in the Land of Not Enough, and these are the coins of the realm.

These magazines and catalogs carry in them the constant message of what we do not have and cannot be. We live in a society that sells us our own unworthiness every day. How can we possibly practice generosity and a belief in abundance amidst a barrage of scarcity?

This is hard, hard work, and one sermon will not get us out of the Land of Not Enough. So I bring you greetings as fellow travelers and word of the place to which we are going. I can bring you a sign that we are growing closer and that our band of travelers grows every day.

Our culture is fascinated with money. We all know the degree to which money is the real religion of America, yet someone recently asked me, "Isn't the first rule of stewardship: Never talk about money?" I was not surprised to hear someone say this, as it's been the practice in churches for a long time. Don't talk with people about money; you'll only make them uncomfortable. Yet I disagree. I think we are longing to talk about money, even in our discomfort.

In church, we grapple with life's most profound matters: justice, death, the nature of humanity, even the existence or non-existence of God. Still, the subject of money rarely comes up. In many churches, it is easier to talk about sex than finances. Yes, we speak of poverty and global economics, and perhaps we share our concerns about paying for retirement. But when do we speak of our deepest worries and fears, about the making and spending of our money?

Each of us has questions. In a culture that shapes us to be consumers before anything else, how do we make financial choices that are in line with our own values? How do we teach our children life's meaning in a society that emphasizes appearances and accumulation? What is our responsibility to the poor? What if *I* become poor?

These are profoundly religious questions, questions of ethics, human worth, and security. And church is the best place for these discussions, when we are gathered with others who share our values. Our congregations can provide a place to examine our materialist culture, to speak truthfully about our questions and struggles, perhaps even to be vulnerable in these questions, and to comfort and encourage one another along the way. This is the first step of religious stewardship.

The next step of stewardship is one that all the great religions have taught through the ages. What if I told you that I know a fantastic spiritual practice, a teaching passed down through millennia, which is the best antidote to depression, cynicism, and malaise? It is a transformative practice, one that will connect you to all living things and offer you a freer heart and boundless joy. You would be begging me to teach you this practice.

And what if I told you this practice was tithing? That's right, the practice of giving a percentage of your material goods back to the religious community. What would you say then?

The world gives us the message that we must look out for our own interests, that life is a race won by the most competitive. The world says that there are limited resources, a finite amount of wealth, goods, and love, and that each of us is on our own as we try to grab what we can. In a world such as this, tithing is a subversive act.

I have tithed for nearly ten years, and it gives me a profound spiritual freedom and grace. Tithing tells me that the income I earn—large or small—does not define who I am. Tithing teaches me, over and over, about my dependence upon others and theirs upon me. Ultimately, it teaches me to place my trust in something other than money, to understand that my security does not lie in material things but rather in community.

The offering is an ancient religious rite, performed in nearly every human society. Whether it was their finest lamb, sheaves of wheat, or wine, people brought to the common altar a portion of their harvest to sustain the wider community. Even the poorest carried something to the table, participating in this reminder of human interdependence.

Our modern version of the offering is manifested each Sunday morning when we pass baskets to support the church's mission. Each of us receives from that shared wealth, and our wider community is also strengthened. Our offerings are less tangible now—dollars and checks instead of grains and livestock. But it is the work of our hands, nonetheless. It is our hard work made into currency. And those hours of work have power: the power to provide, to grow, to shape our world, to build things that will outlast generations.

Now, I have a confession to make. I'm jealous of the Religious Right. I'm jealous of its strength. I'm jealous of its organizing power. I'm jealous of its ability to affect elections, from school boards to presidential campaigns. Is anyone else jealous?

And you know, frankly, I'm jealous of its clarity of purpose. That clarity makes it possible for its proponents to commit themselves wholeheartedly to the pursuit of their values in the world. They have a vision of our nation's future, and they give willingly, joyfully, gratefully of their time, energy, and money to fulfill that vision.

What motivates these religious people to give so deeply? They believe that their values are in danger in these times. They believe that their families are threatened, their worldview is under attack, and their god is defiled. And so, perceiving themselves under attack, they work diligently against that threat. They protect and educate their children; they build institutions to preserve and spread their values; they fund candidates; and they build camps and churches and youth centers and colleges.

I'm jealous.

Where do these mostly working class people find the resources for such a unified effort? Oh, my dear friends . . . they tithe. They give 10 percent of their income to their local churches, and then they give on top of that to affiliated organizations. They believe that God calls them to do so and that giving in this way offers God glory.

The thing is, our God—the force of love in the universe, the unnamable yet ever-present divine spirit of life, the God of trees and rivers and bears, the God of the poor and dispossessed, the God of refugees and hungry children, the God of Thoreau and Emerson, Channing and Parker, Francis David, and all the nameless martyrs of our faith—our God deserves glory too. Our children need protection, our values are under attack, and we must work diligently to defend them against threat.

Some people might say that the purpose of church is to improve ourselves, to teach us spiritual practices, but not to be involved in social matters. I would offer a challenge to those people, for religion holds a unique role in society. Communities of faith perform a singular function. They have what sociologists call an *alternative imagination*, an ability to posit a future different from, and better than, the present we know today.

Our religion describes a future in which every child is fed and warm and sleeps in a dry bed, in which all people are free from want and oppression and despair. And our faith calls us to work for that future.

The church, at its best, is the conscience of the people. As Oscar Romero, the martyred archbishop of El Salvador, once said, the Church "has no intention of being the people's opium. . . . The church wants to rouse men and women to the true meaning of being a people." As Mike Durall puts it, church asks us whether we live our lives any differently than our unchurched neighbors and friends.

We come together on Sunday mornings not just to heal our own souls but also to offer healing outward in the world. Here we learn what it means to be a people working together for the common good.

Now, lest you think churches lack any real power, let me share with you a simple fact. There was not one successful social movement in the United States that did not use religious people as its organizing base. Every successful social movement involved churches and synagogues. Think of the role of churches in the Civil Rights movement or in the Sanctuary movement of the 1980s. There have been other movements too: temperance, women's suffrage, abolition.

There are examples from other countries, as well. Remember the involvement of the church in El Salvador, Nicaragua, and elsewhere, when priests, nuns, and lay people risked everything in the struggle against military dictatorship. Or the simple Hungarian minister, Laszlo Tökes, whose refusal to keep silent ignited the Romanian revolution against the dictator Ceausescu; the revolution in the Philippines against Marcos; the Solidarity movement in Poland, of which John Paul II was an outspoken supporter.

Think also of those times when churches have been silent in the face of evil. Most noteworthy were the churches in Germany during the Third Reich, who through a combination of fear, complicity, and their own anti-Semitism did not speak out against Nazi atrocities.

The Religious Right understands the power to be harnessed in congregations. It is brilliant in its organizing methods. It asks its people to live their faith with conviction.

Think now. Where is the voice of our faith needed to counter injustice and prejudice? What does our Unitarian Universalist faith ask us to do and be in these times? How will we respond?

The great Unitarian theologian and ethicist James Luther Adams said often that in order for goodness to triumph, it must be institutionalized. If we are to make changes in the world, to create a just society, we must organize ourselves. We must lend our voices to the cause of mercy and peace. We must use all our resources—our energy, our time, and our money—to create that society.

So often we decry the power of the Religious Right and wish our own message of love and freedom could be heard, yet we have only begun to lift our voice in the world. Our times demand of us a new fidelity to our faith, and that fidelity requires us to live in new ways. It asks us to be bold, to be strong, and to grow in generosity. We, who statistically have so much more than the rest of the world, are called to serve the good by living generously.

You have a mission: You are hoping to shine the light of our liberal faith here in this community. We need your voice here; there are so many who could find a home with you. And so, as you consider your pledge to this congregation, let me ask you a question. What is the Spirit asking you to give of your resources to the ministry of love and justice? What percentage of your resources does Love ask you to share?

Let me ask you another question. What gift can you give that will be meaningful to you, that will give you strength and clarity in the months ahead? What gift would be exciting and nourishing to your own spirit?

This is how we should give. The old proverb about the Lord loving a cheerful giver is often misunderstood. It doesn't mean that we should give an amount that is easy for us. It doesn't mean you should grin and bear it! It means that we should give a gift that gladdens our hearts, that gives us joy. It means that when we give generously, with authenticity and integrity, the Divine moves in us. The Divine moves in us.

The question is whether we want to live our lives fearfully, trapped in the consumer mindset of our era, or to live lives that are full and free, lives that give us a sense of purpose and wonder.

My friends, I believe it is our best hope, and a sign from the Land of Enough, that you here and our friends in congregations all over this nation are engaged in these questions. This work of generosity outlasts the yearly fund drive and calls us into a deeper communion with each other and with the world. It calls us to be larger, stronger, and braver than we ever imagined we could be.

Do not fear, though, for we are called together. We have one another. These are the ancient tasks of religious people: to trust the wonder of the universe, to use our lives to serve the good, and to be a blessed comfort to one another on the journey.

May it be so, my friends.

Amen.

~

Personal Reflection

Cecelia Kingman Miller asks, "In a culture that shapes us to be consumers before anything else, how do we make financial choices that are in line with our own values?" Consider your own financial choices. Are they in line with your values?

For the Congregation

1. Does giving in your congregation "gladden the hearts" of your members and friends? If so, what have you done to create that feeling? If not, can you imagine an annual canvass, a celebration service, or a way of talking about gifts that would cheer the soul?

2. Cecelia Kingman Miller envies the "clarity of purpose" of the Religious Right. If we liberal religionists articulated our purpose with clarity, what would it sound like? When do you do that in your congregation, and can you do it more often?

STAND BY THIS FAITH

REV. NAOMI KING
Horizon Unitarian Universalist Church
Carrollton, Texas

"Gleaning," as Naomi King says in this challenging sermon, "is hard work." It is the finding and collecting of everything useable after the easy harvesting is done. We aren't used to gleaning because most of our lives are so filled with abundance that we don't have to attend to "the spare strands of wheat that remain on the ground behind the cutting."

But as King leads us through the liberating Biblical tale of Ruth, she casts a new light on Boaz, Ruth's would-be savior. Although he is wealthy, he can't just buy Ruth's freedom without gleaning. In seeking everything useable for Ruth's sake, he too is gathered up, gleaned by love.

In generosity, we find ourselves. We commit ourselves and are even willing to ask others to do the same. Boaz must "stretch his pride" and ask a friend for help to free Ruth. Similarly, Naomi King asks us to get involved in the liberating work of generosity in service of our congregations and our faith. And she asks us to call on others to do the same.

It is up to each of us and comes down to this: Are we willing to be gleaned for love? —T. S.

THE QUESTION FOR US today is, What does it mean for us to stand with our faith, for us to stand with this church?

This is not a new question or one unique to Unitarian Universalists. But the answer to this question almost always means going against conventional wisdom, bucking social trends and peer expectations.

If we look for proof of the age of this answer, we can find many stories from around the world. But the one I come back to, time and time again, is the Book of Ruth. See, the Book of Ruth begins with three women, Orpah, Ruth, and Naomi, who have lost everything—their husbands, their social standing, their homes, their means to make a living, a chance for children. And in their society, this is clearly a sign that they are not blessed. In fact, in their culture, it is widely believed that Orpah, Ruth, and Naomi must have sinned because God somehow forgot to buy them social security—a stable family, lots of children, and a means to make a living.

In that time and place, Ruth and Orpah essentially belong to Naomi; they enter the family and they cannot leave. Naomi could demand that they do everything in their power to make her comfortable and to care for her. But she does not. Instead, in her last powerful act, in the tiny space allotted to her, she says to Orpah and Ruth, "Don't stay with me because that is not fair or right to you; the only future you have with me is slavery." Naomi knows that she has to return to her husband's village and that along with his property, she will be sold to pay his debts. If Orpah and Ruth go with her, they will be sold too.

The question for Naomi is: What is a faithful act? To drag these suffering women with her into slavery, or, in her last free moment, to liberate them to follow their hearts and destinies? Set them on the road to be social outcasts with the attendant shame and suffering, a status considered by many of the time worse than slavery, or invite them into a path of slavery with its sufferings, including the expectation that as women, they could be sexually used by others?

Orpah and Ruth both have to think about this troubling gift Naomi makes. They care about her. They are worried for her. They know the choices they are facing. To go home is to choose a path of suffering, and to enter slavery is to choose a path of suffering. They could also choose to die. But then they listen to their hearts and go where they are called. Orpah returns to her family, and Ruth says to Naomi, "Whatever happens to you will happen to me."

Each makes a *free* choice, a choice for life, and each chooses the path she can best approach. Both know they are bucking conventional wisdom in choosing to follow their hearts and continue to live their lives with caring and love. They know there will be sacrifice and work ahead of them, but even if the suffering is inevitable, the choice is freely made. They set out on faith that goodness has to go beyond social convention, and their actions speak even more loudly than their words as they choose to live and deal with what life has sent their way. What is holy and sacred for them is the right to make these choices. All three women are making generous, difficult sacrifices.

After this, we lose Orpah's side of the story and only follow Ruth and Naomi as they head into sure slavery and degradation. They return to Naomi's husband's village where they seek shelter inside the city wall and Ruth goes out to glean in the fields. Now, I don't know how many of you have ever gleaned; it's not much in vogue with these days of mechanical harvesters that take every last bit of grain, even from the edges of the fields. Gleaning is hard work. You have to fight with the birds and the mice for the spare strands of wheat that remain on the ground and behind the cutting. Gleaning also happens along the edges of the field, where one tenth of the land is set aside for the needs of the destitute. This set-aside land is a sign that the owner of the field recognizes his religious obligation to care for the poor and the destitute.

Boaz, whose field we find Ruth gleaning, has dutifully set aside his tenth of land—a tenth of his income—demonstrating that he is a generous man who puts his money where his prayers are and provides for the needs of the poor. He watches Ruth work hard, and he is taken with the choices she keeps making, choices he understands as being faith-full, not just adhering to the letter of the law. He is so moved by Ruth's choices that he makes a faith-full choice too. He shares with Ruth how much he wants to help. She becomes very excited about the possibility and tells Naomi, who also is excited by what Boaz offers.

But then comes the estate sale the next day, where Ruth and Naomi are to be sold along with the rest of Elimelech's estate. It is the end of their hope for freedom. But Boaz has another problem. He does not have the money to buy out Elimelech's debt and set Ruth and Naomi free. Thus, he must ask his friend for help. Boaz' friend is interested in Elimelech's land; maybe he has a lot of children to divide his estate when he dies. But he has no use for the women who are part of that package. So Boaz is given charge of them. Asking for help from his friends, asking a friend to make a free choice for generosity, requires Boaz to stretch his pride and to be so generous as to incur a major social debt. Because he does so, however, his friend buys out Naomi's husband's debt, and Boaz sets both Naomi and Ruth free. This allows Boaz and Ruth to marry and provide a home for Naomi. Slavery turns toward freedom, and death turns toward life on the basis of making free choices, practicing generosity of heart, and listening to where we are called. The choice, even when it means hard work and sacrifice, is always for freedom to listen to the heart's voice calling.

You have listened to your own heart's voice to come to this place. Whether you were raised Unitarian Universalist, in another tradition, or in no specific tradition, you have made and continue to make a choice to buck conventional wisdom and work in this faith, to follow your heart here. Sometimes that free choice is translated as loyalty, but we have different cultural understandings about loyalty. Loyalty is the description usually given to Ruth. But when, today, we talk about Ruth being loyal to Naomi, we probably imagine something like a balloon on a string and the string just following that balloon around; we don't imagine the *difficult choices* and the *discernment* required. In order for us really to grasp the meaning of loyalty in our faith, this element of discerning must be present, not just following a tether.

The Reverend A. Powell Davies once observed,

> There is and always has been a premium upon an individual's remaining with the loyalties he grew up with. If his family were Baptists who lived in Texas and vote for a certain political party, he will find life easier if he remains a Baptist and a Texan . . . and votes for that same political party. . . . Loyalty is supposed to be best evidenced by remaining with whatever you started out with.
>
> But this is neither sound American principle nor good religion. The founding fathers started out as British subjects and ended up as American citizens; many of them belonged to the Church of England and yet became Unitarians. They not only declared themselves free, they used their freedom to follow their convictions. . . .
>
> What kind of loyalty was this? It was the one loyalty...that is alive and authentic. For the truth is that in the end loyalty is never an attachment to something external so much as it is an allegiance to something inside yourself. That which commands you outwardly has first possessed you inwardly. . . . There is no surer test than this: Your loyalty will always be to what you secretly love and serve.

The challenge for us is to make sure we are providing evidence of what we love and serve, more than secretly. Actions speak louder than words. Do we care about conventional wisdom more than justice? Do we care about keeping up with our neighbors more than enlarging on those who are truly our neighbors and inviting all persons to the party? Where are our hearts leading us, not just in secret, but here, publicly?

This challenge means we are talking about vocation—a calling to something. Here we are, having covenanted with one another, having promised to affirm and promote these principles and draw upon these many traditions. Here we are, answering this calling which sometimes we might struggle to define, answering this calling *here*, to work in *this* church and in *this* faith. Parker Palmer, an educator who has greatly influenced Unitarian Universalist approaches to religious education, once wrote, "Vocation at its deepest level is not, 'Oh, boy, I get to go to this strange place where I have to learn a new way to live and where no one, including me, understands what I'm doing.' Vocation at its deepest level is, 'This is something I can't not do, for reasons I'm unable to explain to anyone else and don't fully understand myself but that are nonetheless compelling.'" That's what Ruth, Naomi, Boaz, and Orpah are responding to. That's what our pantheon of great Unitarian and Universalist and Unitarian Universalist women and men have responded to over the ages.

We are called in this church to use our hearts and hands and minds to bring hope to each other, to pick up despair and hug it into tears, to continue to invite every person to the party because oh, wow, is our dancing good, and isn't our music wonderful? We are first and foremost listening to where our hearts are calling us, checking out that call with our minds, and putting our bodies to work.

Knowing where we are called, and to what meaningful work, and to which relationships is an amazing, life-affirming gift. It would be an amazing experience and a great gift if these calls happened only once in our lives. But even more generously, even more amazingly, they don't just happen once, but repeatedly, every time we're tested and every time something about us changes.

When we go to the dry cleaners and someone asks about where we go to church, do we make the choice to talk about our faith and how wonderful it is? When we meet a friend or a stranger as we go through our daily lives, as we commit to practices that make hope *real* in this world, are we talking about it? Are we acting and speaking in unison? Listening to what calls us to the hope, here and now, is an ongoing spiritual practice and it requires courage and discipline.

When we want to look at courage and discipline, let's look at our youth. In this church, in this movement, we care about our youth. Our youth sometimes are the touch-point for how difficult standing by our faith can be; how many of our children and youth come home having lost their friends because they do not believe in hell and so have just been sentenced to hell on earth for that unbelief? How do we help our young people develop an identity, a rock of faith, from which they can stand and speak and act deeply and fully? We do so through worship and youth camps and YRUU—Young Religious Unitarian Universalists—and religious education programs. But we also do so by talking with our youth about our faith and about their own developing faith, applauding the courage they show in living faith-full lives, and in modeling that same courage and discipline ourselves.

It is work. It is work for our teens and for our children and for our elders and for ourselves because living faith-full lives requires courage and stamina. It requires courage because we are bucking conventional wisdom just being here. The more we give ourselves to hope and act on that, the more we are working against the conventional wisdom.

The conventional wisdom says,

Only a few people are worth caring about, so get everything
for yourself that you can.
If you aren't wealthy, it's your fault.
If you aren't happy, it's your fault.
And you better hope to get to heaven some day.

You are here, though, here where we say,

Everyone is worth caring about, even if we have to struggle
to see that.

We can have enough money and time and give to others too.
There is such a thing as social inequity, and we're working to
change that.
Happiness requires a great many things, and it begins here
in human connection and caring.
And whether there is a heaven or not, we need to get to work
here and now.

What we do here extends beyond these doors, throughout
everything we do and touch in our entire lives. We're doing
church even when we're not at church. We're doing church the
other six days of the week. We're doing church everywhere we go,
every moment. We are making the choice constantly to stand with
this faith and to make hope real.

Standing with this faith, we are living out what we say—that
no punishment, nothing, is worse than conspiring in our own
diminishment, conspiring in our own enslavement to conventional wisdom. We are making a choice for freedom. We are
declaring and dancing and witnessing that no victory is greater
than that which comes when we work to enlarge the circle of
who is included, when we reach out a hand and shoulder to one
another, when we attend to those are hurting. When we move
beyond the *us/them* to a truly universal *we*, when we open this
circle, we are standing with this faith.

Every time you work for this church and write a check, add or
delete a budget line, make no mistake about it—you are living
your faith. Is your faith smaller or greater? Are we here as an
enduring, real, growing presence of hope, making difficult decisions and risking and reaching out? Are we making the choices to
follow our hearts, to find and expand freedom, to be loyal to our
faith? Are we choosing freedom over slavery? Are we asking for
help from our friends, finding some way where there is no apparent way? This is work, difficult work, as difficult as gleaning, as
difficult as the choices of Ruth, Boaz, Orpah, and Naomi. Are we
putting our money where our mouth is?

Oh, that pesky money part! One more story about this, the story of a Southern evangelist who says to his flock, "Brothers and sisters, there's work to be done. Great good to be got. But first we got to take that first little step. And then the second. Then we got to walk together, and not grow weary."

"Amen," said the congregation. Now, every time the congregation says, "Amen" in this story, it would help if you all would offer an "Amen."

"We got to run together, and not grow faint."

"Amen." [The congregation responds, "Amen."]

"We got to spread our wings like eagles and fly!"

"Amen." [The congregation responds, "Amen."]

"But," said the preacher, "we all know today it takes money to fly!"

There were a few scattered "Amens" but mostly silence. And then a voice piped up from the back, "Then let's walk, preacher!"

But here's the truth. If you have the capacity to give generously, know that money is an important way to stand with this church and this faith. I used to recruit board members for non-profit organizations, and when I was out there looking, I looked for three things to show me that someone really was passionate and committed. I found that people who were passionate and committed gave time, invited strangers and friends to the community, and gave what money they could afford to give or raised it from others who could give. It's canvass time, when you're thinking about your pledging and what you want from this Unitarian Universalist faith and from this church. We're not going to get there without you. We need each and every one of you to make hope real.

I know you have the passion; I can feel that. I know your hearts have called you to be in this place; I can see that. I know you have time and are committing that. I know you're going to write the largest check you can and support this faith that is supporting you. I know you're making hope real each and every day. It's your hands that are making hope real, your hands that are gleaning hope from the fields of despair. It's your hands that are changing this world. It's your hands that are employing choices for this world, not deferring them for some heavenly payment.

It is up to you. Separately, we can do a lot. Together, we can make miracles happen.

~

Personal Reflection

Naomi King suggests that loyalty or faithfulness involves being willing to bear witness to our Unitarian Universalist beliefs and values. Do you agree? In which contexts are you most challenged in doing so? Your child's school? Your local professionals' group? Your neighborhood? Why? What liberates you, like Ruth and Boaz, to make your most faithful choices?

Most of us are, at some time, tempted to sell ourselves into a version of slavery, whether it is to an addiction, a lifestyle, a relationship, or something else. What are your personal temptations and how can you best resist them?

For the Congregation

1. Are we automatically "living our faith" by being involved in a congregation? When and in which circumstances does your congregation most seem to reach that standard?
2. If you could choose one way in which your congregation would live its faith with conviction in the future, what would that be? What would it take, now, for you to set off on that path?
3. Imagine that your congregation has just reached the end of your ideal fund drive. What results do you see? How do you know you are living your faith?

Wanting, Getting and Giving

Bonnie McClish Dlott

Mt. Diablo Unitarian Universalist Church
Walnut Creek, California

Whether we like it or not, most of us struggle with consumerism. In fact, the greatest impediment to giving generously may well be our fear of not having enough. In order to give joyfully from our limited resources, we need to confront that fear and realize what a seductive demon it is.

In this engaging sermon, Bonnie McClish Dlott invites us not only to meet our fear but, more importantly, to uncover the true source of spiritual abundance. With a touch that is simultaneously light and serious, she shares her own experience with the seduction of shopping, a compulsion with which most of us have had some experience. Then she helps us find the place in our lives where giving becomes transforming.

The issues of this sermon—getting, having, and giving—are the fundamental emotional and spiritual issues of stewardship. The sermon itself is a generous creation in which the author is willing to make herself vulnerable that she might touch something universal for the rest of us. She succeeds with grace. –S. M.

LAST SPRING, I GOT A MESSAGE from the universe. Now, I do not get too many messages from the universe; sometimes I do not even get my phone messages. But this message was very loud, and it came at four in the morning in the form of a tremendous thud from my closet. This particular message was one that my husband had tried to send me several times, but I had managed to ignore him. Messages from the universe, on the other hand, are not so easily dismissed. They are not like Post-It notes that you can throw away. They tend to be big messages, like "Your life is too stressful," or "It's time to find a new career."

This was one of those big messages. The message was, "You have too many clothes." The stupendous weight of my clothes pulled the bracket holding the closet rod right off the shelf it was attached to, and my beautiful wardrobe hit the floor. I was stunned. Hadn't I just gone through this closet and taken out a few dozen things to give away? How could this happen?

My recent wardrobe purge was the result of a class I took in seminary last semester about stewardship. Some of the early sessions focused on American consumerism and how it hurts our pocketbooks, our environment, and even our souls. We did an exercise that included a visualization of our living space, and we tried to imagine what we would take out if we had ten minutes to grab things before our house burned down. I had trouble thinking of anything that I would take except my photographs and the videotapes of my children. The thought of carrying out clothing hadn't even crossed my mind. I started to ask myself questions. If my clothes don't mean that much to me, why do I own so many?

I suspect that this is a good question for all of us to think about. We make more money than we ever have as a nation, and we buy more things, yet we save much less than our parents and grandparents did. We carry staggering amounts of credit card debt, and more and more of us go bankrupt each year. Why do we buy so much stuff?

I thought about this as my husband fretted about the closet repair. Why do I have so many outfits? Hey, I know the answer to this question: because I want them! I see something on the rack, and I fall in love. My heart pounds as I search for the right size. I start to breathe heavily as I try it on. Look at me: I look so . . . whatever—professional, sexy, smart, cool, tough, hip! It's like magic; I'm transformed into a new person in this outfit, and I like what I see! If I just had this outfit, I would feel good about myself. Each piece of clothing is a transformational opportunity.

My spouse announced that it was time for a pilgrimage to Home Depot. I felt so guilty about my clothes that I agreed to go with him. We drove there and navigated through the jammed parking lot, desperately vying for a space with several hundred other people, all just as anxious as we were to buy things. We walked down aisles towering with merchandise, and as usual, I began to feel over-whelmed by the transformational opportunities I saw. Here is an opportunity to be transformed into a person with perfect kitchen countertops. Here is an opportunity to be transformed into a person with hardwood floors. How about an opportunity to be transformed into a person with a beautiful yard? I could be so happy!

Luckily, my husband was on a mission and just wanted to be transformed into a person who could hang his few shirts up in a closet that was supposedly half his. He picked out some braces that looked like they could hold up an entire circus tent, and we headed to the cashier. We managed to get out of the store and back home without incident, and by the end of the day, my clothes were hanging up again.

This wasn't the end of the story for me. I was starting to feel that I understood my own wanting; it had to do with becoming someone improved, someone I liked better than who I was without the item. Yet, I had to ask myself in the case of my wardrobe: Had I actually become someone better once that new outfit was in my possession? Had that happy feeling persisted past one or two washings? Even more importantly, what was it about myself that needed transforming, and how is real transformation accomplished? Can it be accomplished by getting things?

I tried to think back to significant transformations in my life. Most of them happened as a result of a lifelong commitment—to my partner, my children, or to my work in ministry. Each of these commitments involved wanting and getting, but as I thought, I began to understand that I hadn't been transformed from wanting and getting. I had been transformed by the giving that had happened after the wanting and getting. For example, I wanted the love and security of a life partner, and I got it, but what transformed me wasn't the getting; it happened later, in the giving, in learning that I was capable of making sacrifices and working with my spouse to make a life together.

The wanting and the getting of children was not particularly transformational for me, well, at least not permanently. It was later, in the giving, and giving, and giving, that the transformation happened. When my children were young, I learned that I was stronger than I thought I was, more patient than I thought I was, and capable of feeling more love than I had ever dreamed of. I learned that I could put someone else's interest ahead of my own and that I could be counted on. Most importantly, I learned that even though I was not perfect and never would be, I was loved and needed. All this I learned not from wanting or getting, but by giving.

My path into the ministry is yet another example. When my second child was born, I realized that I had everything I had ever wanted, yet I wasn't really happy. In the years that followed, I searched for the missing *thing* that would do the trick. It won't surprise you to hear that the *thing* that I needed was the opportunity to use my gifts to express my love for life within a community. After the wanting and the getting, I needed to give myself back— to my partner, to my family, and now to my Unitarian Universalist community and movement.

So now you know about some of my struggles with wanting, getting, and giving, mostly as it applies to my energy and time, but I'd like to get back to my wardrobe. It cost a lot of money, yet it has very little actual worth to me. My Old Testament teacher would tell me that it was "idolatrous," that the money I spent on it was spent for my own glorification and thrill. I'd have a hard time arguing with him. Wouldn't it have been nice if I had spent that money on something that was more meaningful, something that reflected my values as a Unitarian Universalist?

I think it's hard to talk about money, and maybe to some, a discussion of money seems out of place in church. I don't agree. Money is something that means a lot to us, and so does our faith. I believe that the way we use money should have something to do with our faith. As Unitarian Universalists, we are no different than folks in other denominations. We need money to pay for our food, our shelter, our clothes. We need to save for our children's education and for our retirement. We give some of it away to our church and some to other good causes.

We are different, however, in two important ways. Unitarian Universalists make more money than people in other denominations, and we give less of it away. I worry about this. All religions stress the importance of generosity. After all my reflections about wanting, and getting, and giving, I start to wonder. Are we hurting ourselves by not giving? Are we missing a real transformational opportunity?

I know that sitting in this room now are some exceptional people that do give to our churches and to other charities very generously, perhaps so generously that they have to make sacrifices in other areas in their lives. Maybe they want things, but they don't buy them because it is more important to them to be generous to this church or to others. Here is what I want to know. What is it that they are getting by giving that is so important to them? What am I missing out on with my comfortable pledge? Could I risk giving up something to find out?

My first impulse is to say, "No! I already give to the church, and I don't want to deprive myself of something I want. It will feel uncomfortable to want something and not to get it." Then I think of a conversation that we had in my stewardship class. We talked about how it might feel to invite people from our struggling partner church in Transylvania into our homes. I imagine showing them my closet bursting with clothes and my refrigerator stuffed with food and fine wine, and then I imagine saying to them, "I'm sorry, but I just can't afford to help you to feed and house your minister or help you to buy a cow so your children can have fresh milk. I can't afford to help you, because I need to buy myself more clothes so I can feel happy for a few days."

When I imagine that scenario, I feel far worse than I would just passing on a great outfit. I understand that wanting and getting things don't really transform me at all. In fact, I suspect that wanting and getting might be preventing me from becoming the person I long to be.

Who is that person? One way to find out is to ask myself, "How do I want to be remembered?" I can just see the obituary now. Loving daughter, wife, and mother; she was a snappy dresser. I would much rather read that my life-long commitment to giving reflected the love that I felt for life and for Unitarian Universalism. I hope that others will be inspired when they read that I tithed to the church I served and left part of my estate to the Unitarian Universalist Association. I don't want to leave as a legacy for my children the ideal of wanting and having. It wasn't enough for me, and I know that it won't be enough for them either.

I would like to ask you to think about some questions this week. What things do you own, and what do they mean to you? Do you have so many things that you can't fit them all into your home? How much more do you think you need to buy to be happy? Is wanting and getting enough for you? What would you give up to feed someone who is hungry? Does your checkbook register accurately reflect your faith and principles? Who is the person that you want to be, and how does that person spend his or her time and money? Are you ready to be transformed into that person?

Let me end by saying that the message I received from the universe turned out to be a message of hope. The message was, "You have enough to make a difference." If I can make a difference, then together, we Unitarian Universalists can make a big difference. I believe that if we are willing to look carefully at our lives and give as generously as we can, we can be transformed into the people and the movement that we dream of being. We can bring our life-affirming vision of love and justice into a world that so desperately needs it. That is my hope, and my dream, and it is worth more to me than anything I could buy.

May you go in peace, and give your very best this week. Blessed Be.

∽

Personal Reflection

Bonnie McClish Dlott suggests that most of us are seeking spiritual transformation. The question is, "How does real transformation happen?" What is the most important transformation you have experienced in your life? Did either getting or giving play a role?

Fundraisers sometimes talk about "giving until it feels good." What has been the greatest giving you have ever done in your life? Did it result in feeling good spiritually?

For the Congregation

1. If you were going to try to ask the other members of your congregation to give something that would represent a sacrifice for them, what would it be? What difference would it make to the congregation or to the larger world?

2. Bonnie McClish Dlott discusses her own attempts at superficial transformation, such as buying and wearing a new outfit. How, she asks, does real transformation occur? What is the greatest "real" transformation your congregation has ever experienced? What did people have to give for that to happen? What was the result?
3. What real transformation does your congregation need now?

THE SHOEMAKER'S WINDOW

REV. PATRICK T. O'NEILL

First Unitarian Church
Wilmington, Delaware

Like Patrick O'Neill, the majority of Unitarian Universalists are "come-outers," folks who join our congregations as adults. Maybe they were ecclesiastically singed, or maybe they're just looking for a better spiritual fit in their religious homes. Either way, almost all came to us on a personal journey, trying to find a better way of being human religiously.

It makes sense, then, that a lot of people in our congregations think in terms of getting their needs met. At canvass time, it is very tempting to do an evaluation and ask, "Do the sermons feed me? Do my kids want to go to church school? Have I found the church of my dreams?" These are very rational, here-and-now concerns, and they lead to a rational sense of scarcity since no one's needs are ever completely met. There may be "more love somewhere," but individual generosity, approached this way, gives donors the idea that there ought to be more here and now. The great gift of O'Neill's sermon is that he takes us on a journey out from ourselves and into the commonwealth of community.

Ushered into the grandeur of Chartres Cathedral, we are focused on the incredible stained glass windows. The guide comments, "These windows, many of them, were given one mosaic at a time,

piece by piece, coin by coin, by people who wanted to contribute
something beautiful to last the ages."

"To last the ages" requires giving beyond our own needs, toward
times we shall never see. The work of generosity is not about check-
ing the ledger of here-and-now, but about seeing beyond ourselves
into the possibility of more abundant times. As O'Neill puts it, "Here
is what I know about communities of faith: these are precious and
rare, life-changing institutions, these little churches of ours. They
touch people, and they are meaningful in people's lives in ways that
most of us can only guess at, even those of us who have been active
committed leaders ourselves for many years."

Enjoy this wonderful sermon that leads us toward the promised
times. —T. S.

$\sim$

YOUR PRESENCE HERE in such numbers today is a wonderful indicator that this congregation is important to you and to people you
love.

I want to reflect with you just a bit this morning on what it is
about these unique communities called congregations that we
choose to affirm in the first place, and why these little institutions
continue to claim our loyalty over the years.

Let's face it. You probably drove past three or four or five different houses of worship on your way here this morning. I've long
felt that ministers ought to give that same announcement that
flight attendants give when you land at the airport—you know, the
one that says, "We realize that you had a choice of airlines in coming to Washington today, and we thank you for choosing United."
We ought to say, "We realize you had choice of congregations to
attend this morning, and we thank you for choosing this Unitarian
Universalist congregation as your place of worship today!"

It will probably not surprise you to learn that, as a minister, I
have a great personal fondness for churches and temples of all

kinds. I mean, for houses of worship in general, the buildings where religious groups congregate for worship. I love churches and temples, mosques and monasteries, ashrams and chapels of all kinds. From the most grandiose and ornate to the smallest and most humble, I find them all quite fascinating. I always have.

I have never met a professional clergy person yet—minister, priest, rabbi, or imam—who did not have a similar feeling for houses of worship. I imagine we're a bit like surgeons who are fascinated by other people's operating rooms. As my family can tell you, I cannot walk by a new church or a temple without trying the front door to see if I can get a peek inside.

And if perchance the door is open, and I have the opportunity to look around, I prowl all over the place. I'll know everything about it in twenty minutes. I read all the plaques and dedication plates; I read the cornerstones; I sit in the pews; I kneel on the kneelers. If there are candles to be lit, I light a candle in memory of my grandmother, and I say a prayer that she once taught me.

You can tell a lot about a church or a temple just by sitting there quietly by yourself for a few minutes. You can tell a lot just by experiencing the light in the room, the acoustics, and the visual aesthetics—the balance and symmetry of the place. I always try to imagine what kind of people worship there and what kind of God might be honored there.

I try to check out the view from the choir loft, if there is one. And if the place is empty and I can get to it, I always climb up and stand in the pulpit—just for a minute—I don't disturb anything— just to see what it's like, a quick little "test drive" to see how it handles. (I often wonder what I would say if anybody ever caught me doing that in a strange church. Clergy, of course, understand this about each other, but church custodians tend to frown on people trespassing in their pulpits!) To this point in my life, I have been privileged to visit six or seven countries, and I have visited and explored some of the most famous and most beautiful places of worship in the world.

In America, I have visited the Cathedral of St. John the Divine and, of course, St. Patrick's in New York City, and the white marble National Cathedral in Washington. In California, in a redwood forest, I worshipped in a Zen monastery building that was octagonal in shape and made completely by hand of polished rosewood by a Zen Master, who also happened to be a master carpenter.

In Canada, I've been to Notre Dame Church in Montreal, with its ornate hand-carved wooden chancel—that beautiful church of perfect acoustics where Pavarotti's Christmas concert was taped. In Spain, I've stood in the Great Cathedral of Seville, where Christopher Columbus is buried. I visited the Great Mosque in Cordoba, with its one thousand pillars of marble, no two of them the same in design. I have worshipped in Christopher Wren's magnificent Cathedral of St. Paul's and in Westminster in London, where it seems as though every notable in British history is buried.

And, of course, I have been to magnificent Notre Dame in Paris and to St. Chappelle and Sacre Coeur in the City of Light. I've also been to San Marco's in Venice, the Duomo in Florence, and St. Peter's in Vatican City.

I love all these places, and I've had religious experiences literally in all of them. But to one who loves churches, holy places, history, and classical architecture, the most beautiful and impressive of them all, in my opinion, is the eight-hundred-year-old Cathedral of Chartres in France.

Nothing I had read or studied prepared me for the sheer beauty of Chartres. It sits in the midst of an agrarian countryside, fifty miles from Paris, with no city high-rise buildings around it or anywhere near it. As my wife and I approached it one spring day, driving from the south, it rose up ten miles away. We saw it as I imagine pilgrims in the twelfth century saw it as they walked from all over Europe to visit Chartres.

It was an aesthetic experience in every way just to be inside that building. But above all, it was the light, the softness and texture of the light, as it filtered through gorgeous glass windows, stained red and blue and green and gold more than eight hundred years ago, all still vibrant with color. It was the light, above all, that I remember about Chartres, the light from 167 windows in that cathedral, two stories of them—roses, oculi, lancets—each one of those windows a masterpiece of beauty and workmanship, transcending time, transcending space. Some of those windows had faded ever so slightly with the sunlight of eight centuries of summers. Imagine, eight centuries of sunrises and sunsets.

It was the light that I remember in Chartres, what those windows did to it, what they created with it. They wrapped you in color, and they turned the cold hardness of granite stone flooring into a kind of warm, liquid carpet. Those windows were each impossibly beautiful and impossibly intricate, with hundreds of mosaics leaded together to illustrate epic stories from scripture, or stories from the lives of the saints, from the life of Christ, from the prophets, from the history of Christendom.

Each window of a medieval cathedral is a kind of storybook, an artistic rendering for worshippers and pilgrims of a far-off, preliterate culture in the time before printing presses, when faith was transferred through oral teaching, through stories and parables, through music and visual art.

Not far inside the cathedral I found myself standing at the foot of one soaring, magnificent window, with hundreds of pieces of mosaic glass of all colors. It seemed to recount the entire Old Testament; it was so elaborate and exquisite. At the very bottom of the window there was a small frame that showed a cobbler, a shoemaker huddled over his worktable.

Our guide saw me studying this image. "This is the Shoemaker's Window," he explained. "It was installed in 1201 and is considered one of the most beautiful of all. It was a gift from the shoemakers of every village in France, who each contributed whatever they could, even the smallest coins, to commission this work of art for God's house."

The royalty and the wealthiest nobles of France, he continued, gave some of these windows, but this window was a gift of the shoemakers. Another window was given by village water-carriers from all over France. Butchers gave another. Fishmongers gave one. Vine-growers and tanners gave windows in the same manner. As did masons and furriers and drapers, and weavers, coopers, and carpenters and cartwrights. The blacksmiths gave a window, and the milliners gave one, and the apothecaries gave one too. "These windows, many of them," said my guide, "were given one mosaic at a time, piece by piece, coin by coin, by people who wanted to contribute something beautiful to last the ages."

How I wish I could transport every one of you to see those windows in Chartres Cathedral this morning, right now, to see what those working people from little villages all over France were able to give to their church, and hence to all the pilgrims of eight centuries, like me, who have visited there. The irony, as my guide told me, is that these majestic windows, which are the very symbol of medieval greatness in art and architecture and which are beyond value today, were mostly the gifts of common people, not the provenance of the wealthy or the nobility.

As I pondered what I might say to you this morning to get across, in a concrete image, what your support for the church on this Affirmation Sunday means and what your individual place in the life of this congregation means, it was that Shoemaker's Window that kept cropping up in my mind.

When we talk about supporting our churches, in this we are the same: Any congregation, from the largest cathedral to the smallest and plainest chapel, is always the gift of those common people who love it and who work for it and who support it as they are able. It is the love of its congregation that ultimately sanctifies a church or a temple or a meetinghouse and makes of it a sanctuary, a holy place, a community that transcends time.

In twenty-plus years as a minister, time and again, I have been truly humbled by the loving loyalty and the stunning generosity of spirit in which people hold their churches. Two stories, in particular, I'd like to share with you this morning. The first story I tell with the permission of one of my church members. She called me one day a couple of years ago and said she wanted to see me that day. It sounded urgent. Little did I know.

Over a cup of coffee, my friend told me that her family had recently had the good fortune to inherit a large amount of money. They lived modestly, their grown children were all provided for, and she wanted to give the church a gift. "I suppose I could wait till I die to do this, but I'd rather see it do some good for the church." And with that, she gave me a million dollars. "It's an unrestricted capital gift to be used toward a new sanctuary," she said.

She was crying as she announced this to me. When I asked her why she was crying, she said, "Because this feels even better than I thought it would!" To say I was stunned by this incredible gift of generosity is putting it mildly. The two of us sat there crying and laughing into our coffee cups. It was this gift that enabled our church to purchase some adjacent land this year and to make plans for a new sanctuary in the next couple of years.

I want to tell you another story about generosity this morning, one that I shared with the canvass committee the other night. As you might guess from my name, I was not born and raised a Unitarian Universalist. I grew up in an Irish Catholic family, and I first learned a lot of what I know about church community by watching the folks who were part of the working-class Catholic parish where I grew up in New Jersey.

This particular story is about a man in our church named Bill. Bill was an immigrant laborer who worked as a longshoreman on the docks of New York. He lived across the street from the church with his wife and seven children, and he was a devout churchman.

One year (I was probably about ten years old at the time) Bill was laid off work in an extended strike, and he was unable to pay his financial pledge to the church. Now, this was a serious blow to Bill's pride. He knew it was a poor parish that needed all the contributions it could get.

So, as my mother later told the story, Bill went to the pastor and volunteered to contribute his services as the unpaid evening custodian for the church school until he could afford to resume his financial pledge. "It's something the church needs," he said. "And instead of paying for this service, the church can use the money to do good work."

So each evening he worked several hours, for no pay, sweeping and mopping the church school classrooms and hallways and staircases. On snowy days, in those years before snow blowers, Bill got up early to shovel the church school sidewalks before the children arrived for classes. Unable to contribute financially to his church, he found a workingman's way to contribute his fair share.

The dock strike ended some months later, and Bill was once again able to resume his full-time day job and resume his financial pledge to the church. But he decided, in addition to his pledge, to continue working as the unpaid night custodian of the church, which he did for the next thirty years. I know that this story is true because Bill was my father.

Here is what I know about communities of faith: These are precious and rare, life-changing institutions, these little churches of ours. They touch people, and they are meaningful in people's lives in ways that most of us can only guess at, even those of us who have been active, committed leaders ourselves for many years.

A church, finally, is nothing more than its people and what they bring to it—their faith, their vision, their collective hopes and dreams, their memories and their customs, their history, their prayers, their good works and their values. And what community we are able to create here for ourselves is like that great stained-glass window itself, pieced together always with painstaking love and unending patience, each one of us—shoemakers, cobblers, candlestick makers—bringing one more mosaic to the whole.

John Wolf, the minister emeritus of a church in Tulsa, once wrote,

There is only one reason for joining a Unitarian Universalist church and that is to support it. You want to support it because it stands against superstition and fear. Because this church points to what is noblest and best in human life. Because it is open to women and men of whatever race, creed, color, place of origin, or sexual orientation.

You want to support a Unitarian Universalist church because it has a free pulpit. Because you can hear ideas expressed there that would cost any other minister his or her job. You want to support it because it is a place where children come without being saddled with guilt or terrified of some celestial Peeping Tom, where they can learn that religion is for joy, for comfort, for gratitude and love.

You want to support it because it is a place where walls between people are torn down rather than built up. Because it is a place for the religious displaced persons of our time, the refugees from mixed marriages, the unwanted freethinkers, and those who insist against orthodoxy that they must work out their own beliefs.

You want to support a UU church because it is more concerned with human beings than with dogmas. Because it searches for the holy, rather than dwelling upon the depraved. Because it calls no one a sinner, yet knows how deep is the struggle in each person's breast and how great is the hunger for what is good.

You want to support a UU church because it can laugh. Because it stands for something in a day when religion is still more concerned with platitudes than with prejudice and war. You want to support it not because it buys you some insurance policy towards your funeral service but because it insults neither your intelligence nor your conscience, and because it calls you to worship what is truly worthy of your sacrifice. There is only one reason for joining a Unitarian Universalist church—to support it!

This Affirmation Sunday is about each one of us looking inside for what it is that we most treasure and value about our church and making a personal commitment, as we are each able to do so, to empower those values in living community.

A story for you, in closing. It's the story of the Church of Scotland minister, himself a teetotaler, who gave his small highland congregation a scathing, if ineffective, sermon on the evils of alcohol. The following week, he and all his neighbors were invited to a harvest feast at the manor of the area's richest farmer, Lord MacGregor.

Now, Lord MacGregor's farm was famed not only for the prized barley and oats which it produced but also for the fine cherry brandy that old MacGregor himself bottled every year. At the end of the magnificent feast, each guest was served a glass of the cherry brandy. Not wishing to offend his host, the parson did drink his serving and found it to be quite delicious. In fact, as he took his leave that evening, he discreetly asked Lord MacGregor if he might have a case of the brandy donated to the parsonage—strictly for medicinal purposes, of course.

MacGregor was happy to do so, on one condition—that the minister himself write a public thank-you for the gift for the front page of the parish newsletter. The parson thought for a moment and then agreed to do so. The next morning not one but two cases of the cherry brandy were delivered as promised to the parsonage. And as promised, the minister wrote this public thank you in the next newsletter:

> The minister wishes to thank Lord MacGregor for his most generous gift of fruit to the parsonage this week. But even more importantly, we thank the Lord for the fine spirit in which it was offered!

We thank you for the fine spirit in which you support this congregation!

~

Personal Reflection

Patrick O'Neill's sermon challenges us to move beyond thinking of our church simply as a place to get our individual and communal needs met. Indeed, beyond their beauty, the magic of the stained-glass windows at Chartres Cathedral lies in their ability to connect us to the history of human spiritual seeking. Consider the times you think of your religious community as being there to meet your needs. Do those times encourage you to be spiritually generous or spiritually critical? Compare those to the times in which congregational life links you to the long line of thinkers, seekers, and activists who have come before. When does that connection happen for you—special moments of worship, community sharing, social activism? Reflect on how you can make those moments "last forever."

Perhaps the most moving revelation about the Shoemaker's Window is that it was created through the support of common people. Because of those people, others have experienced the beauty and inspiration of Chartres for hundreds of years. Reflect on the contributions you have made—anonymously, humbly, or grandly—that have provided access to spiritual community for others. What might you yet do, great or small, that will help your community last the ages?

For the Congregation

1. The sermon begins with a tour of the speaker's visits to many great houses of worship in the United States and Europe. What feelings of connection to something beyond themselves do you think he might elicit in his Unitarian Universalist listeners?

2. What seems to move Patrick O'Neill most about the Shoemaker's Window? Who might the "shoemakers" in our

congregations be?

3. When the minister's friend offers the generous gift of $1 million to the church, both of them end up crying. What are the deep emotions touched by giving? What does it mean to "give until it feels good"? How does that differ from "giving until it hurts"? Does our subconscious goal ever seem to be to give only so long as we cannot feel it? Does a gift that requires a sacrifice or some change in priorities mean more, spiritually, to both the giver and the recipient?

4. O'Neill's father seems to have initiated his volunteer custodial work to pay off a debt. What do you think he discovered in doing the work that caused him to continue even after he was able to make financial contributions again? If a member of your congregation asked whether he or she can give service instead of money, what would you say? Is it appropriate to say you need both from all who can give them?

5. Read over John Wolf's words on page 35 again. Now, as a group, make a list of all the ways members of your congregation support their church, and the kinds of support that are still needed.

Filthy Lucre or Golden Opportunity?

Rev. Gary Blaine
First Unitarian Church of Toledo
Toledo, Ohio

Many of the sermons in this collection seek to inspire a congregation to support the work of the church, usually at canvass time. Gary Blaine begins with a prior step. Here he teases out the various feelings and conflicts money causes us while acknowledging the importance of money and wealth in our lives. He seeks to liberate us from our guilt and fear.

Blaine says that the greatest impediment to responsible stewardship is our ignorance—not only of our own feelings but also of how to use our money wisely. Thus, an important step in our liberation is learning more both about ourselves and about financial management. It is a challenge worth taking seriously. –S. M.

LAST SUNDAY I SPOKE on the themes of religion, sex, and politics. I thought this morning that I would speak of yet another taboo, money. Unitarian Universalists do not seem to mind if the minister preaches on sex. Religion in light doses is generally acceptable. Politics is often dangerous. But money is the bane of the pulpit. Most ministers only dare to preach the annual "Sermon on the Amount" when the congregation begins its pledge drive for the next fiscal year.

I suppose there are several reasons why money seems to be anathema to ministers and their congregations. I think one of the reasons is found in the naiveté with which many ministers approach the subject. Many are idealistic. Christians have struggled for centuries with what to do with Jesus' command to the young rich man. "Go sell what you own, and give the money to the poor, and you will have treasure in heaven, then come follow me" (Mark 10:21). Many believe that this is a literal command, and a few have thought that Jesus may well have had his tongue planted firmly in his cheek when he said it.

While many wonder what to make of this story, it is the same minister who must come before his or her congregation and beg for more money to raise the budget or pay for the most recent repair bill. The fact of the matter is that many ministers do not know how to read a budget statement or understand concepts as simple as cash flow.

When I taught church administration at Phillips Theological Seminary, very few students were glad to be in the class. Some waited until their senior year to take the required course. Many thought the work of finance and administration was drudgery and not really what they went into the ministry for. At the same time, I have met many lay people who get elected to the church's board of trustees and are disturbed at the amount of time the board spends on finances, personnel, maintenance, and administration. They seldom serve their full terms.

Perhaps there has been too much scandal around money and

church. Jesus threw the moneychangers out of the temple, but we note that he called Judas to be the treasurer for his little band of apostles. The same Judas would betray Jesus for thirty pieces of silver.

If you read the book of Acts carefully you will realize that the very first fight in the Christian church was about money. The question was how to distribute alms to the poor. Some of the widows were not certain that they were getting their fair cut. Money is often the reason why churches are still fighting. The New Testament letters of Timothy and Titus stipulate that bishops must not be greedy for money. Timothy wrote, "For the love of money is a root of all kinds of evil, and in their eagerness to be rich some have wandered away from the faith and pierced themselves with many pains" (I Tim. 6:10). The King James Version uses the term filthy lucre.

Stories abound of ministers who run off with the church's money. There are ministers who equate faith with prosperity or push prayer cloths or religious bric-a-brac in exchange for financial contributions. They offend us mightily. And who can forget the money schemes of Jim and Tammy Faye Bakker and the people who lost their entire life savings because of them?

Churches trust too much, and we want it that way, but when we discover that the funds have been purloined we are disillusioned. Church books are never audited enough, financial and management practices are often questionable, and there never seems to be enough money. Every time you turn around, the church has its hand out for more money. Think of all those book sales, spaghetti suppers, car washes, and bake sales.

There are some people who, quite frankly, are not sure that their gifts to the church earn enough return. Putting money in the offering plate is not like investing in a mutual fund, where slow but certain growth is a reasonable expectation. We are often not sure what the benefits or rewards are for our contributions to the church. There are a number of people who shudder when they realize that over 50 percent of all church budgets are designated for salaries. They are not sure what it is that those people do or why we need them all in the first place.

There are few quantifiable and objective results that are obvious to the average person. These same people might be surprised to know that church professionals and support staff also wonder what good they have done lately and who really appreciates the fifty-hour work weeks they are giving to the congregation. Other people use money as a way to influence the decisions of the church. Some withhold their financial support because they do not like the minister or are angry because the sanctuary was painted antique white instead of cream. They seldom realize that the people who are hurt by withholding a pledge include all of the staff who did not get a raise or whose benefits were curbed.

Another reason why churches are in denial about money is that money is too close to our real values. Ralph Waldo Emerson wrote, "*Political Economy* is as good a book wherein to read the life of a man and the ascendancy of laws over all private and hostile influences, as any Bible which has come down to us." In other words, you cannot determine a person's character by how often he or she opens the Good Book. People's values are more accurately displayed in their checkbook. What we spend our money on speaks volumes about what we really cherish.

We are uncomfortable talking about money because we often feel—or are made to feel—guilty about the fact that, by the world's standards, we are wealthy people. There is not a single person in this room, no matter how modest his or her income, who is not rich in comparison to women and men in third- and fourth-world countries. Most of us will consume more protein in one week than some people will consume in a year. We are sensitive to the suggestion of classism, and we are not certain what to do when the Unitarian Universalist Association exhorts us to economic justice.

The fact of the matter is that the average American family is only three paychecks away from financial insolvency. The greatest stress on most marriages is financial, especially revolving credit debt. American family incomes, adjusted for inflation, are no longer growing. In the 1960s, family incomes grew about 3 percent annually. Since the 1980s, they have not grown at all. We are not certain what to do about the paradox of our relative wealth and precarious financial security. And quite frankly, the church has done little to teach us real stewardship or speak honestly about the place of money in our lives.

The church's stewardship campaign is about the church's money and seems remote from our personal finances. We get the message that we should give more, while the church seems out of touch with our financial realities. Robert Wuthnow, one of the best sociologists of religion in America, has persuasively argued that American churches are in economic crisis, especially with the gap between revenue and expenditures. "Revenues are dropping off," wrote Wuthnow, "especially when giving is adjusted for inflation or is considered in relation to family incomes. Just as this decrease is happening, the need for resources has never been greater. Increasing numbers of disadvantaged people are looking to the churches for help. The churches are being asked to fill the gaps left by cuts in government welfare programs. Staff salaries are squeezed. Old buildings are in disrepair. New congregants are needed." This description reveals not only the struggle of First Unitarian Church of Toledo on Collingwood Boulevard but that of most of the other churches on Collingwood Boulevard as well.

There are two reasons why we are in this predicament, and both reasons are related. The first is that most people are struggling with their own financial needs and do not see how the church is related to them. The church has not taken seriously the stewardship of families and how her families may prosper financially. The average family does not see a relationship between its own financial struggles and the ministry of the church. The second issue is the failure of the church to help people connect their money with their values—their hard-earned incomes with the characteristics of life they deem important. There is a spiritual malaise in our congregations because we have disconnected our financial security from our most cherished convictions.

I do not propose to solve this problem in one sermon. I do propose to initiate a conversation that will lead us to a stewardship of our best Unitarian Universalist principles with our financial well-being. I propose that we bless money talk and agree that we will engage in it. This means that we can plan religious education that promotes financial well-being in the families of our parish. We can teach people about budgets that reflect their values and their dreams. We can teach people techniques, such as debt stacking, to work their way out of debt. We can teach people that living means giving and how we can do that and pay for our children's college education. It means that we can talk openly and honestly about our church's financial needs, how to manage our endowment responsibly, and how we can expand the ministry of the church to meet the spiritual needs of future generations.

As a modest beginning, let me state that money is *not* evil. Wealth is *not* evil. Earning money or gaining wealth is *not* evil. Indeed, to eliminate money would require the demise of human civilization and a return to the Bronze Age. The fact of the matter is that each of us is a consumer. From the moment we are conceived, we consume. Is it even possible to calculate fully how much food and water we consume, the clothes we require, the shelter we demand, the education we esteem, and the health care we necessitate?

Emerson suggested that, by our very human constitution, we are expensive and we thus need to be rich. This is what it means to be a human being, and it requires that we must make money to secure the expensive habit of being alive. If we do not, we are faced with the terrible agony of begging for food, suffering, starving, being exposed to the elements, and wandering lost without friends. This is the nature of things; indeed, it amounts to one of those natural laws that not one of us can escape.

But the fact of the matter is, few people are satisfied with subsistence living. Beans and bread in a lowly tenement building hardly satiates the human hunger for knowledge, modern conveniences, even the arts. I have never met a person living in Section VIII housing who was content to stay there. Everyone dreams of owning his or her own home. Most people I know who live in school districts that are failing would move quickly to a better suburban school if they could afford it, or they would put their children in a private school. I have never known parents who did not seek the best advantages they could possibly obtain for their children. Loyalty to race, or the city, or the old neighborhood quickly fades with the possibility of economic or educational advantage. I submit to you that all of us are inclined to seek the best for ourselves and our families. It is natural, and I dare submit that it follows some natural law, to protect and provide for our young.

If our religious or political ideologies have suggested that the quest for financial security and well being are misguided, wrong, or sinful, I submit that such ideologies violate a realistic understanding of human nature. They will inevitably fail. It is not money—or the quest for money—that disrupts and distorts us. It is the idolatry of money, or the gain of money by corrupt means, that is wrong. Human beings become broken when we worship the golden calf or our stocks and bonds. King Midas was a fool who became greedy and valued everything against the standard of gold, even the life of his daughter. *Lucre* simply means gain or wealth, but it becomes *filthy lucre* when it is achieved by oppression, usury, theft, fraud, or extortion. "Society is barbarous until every industrious man can get his living without dishonest customs," said Mr. Emerson.

Money provides opportunities for us to better our own condition and enjoy the finer fruits of life. We can make our own place in the world, live within our means, and at the same time contribute to the common good of all persons. We cannot speak about the UU Principle affirming the inherent worth and dignity of every person if that person cannot sustain his or her family. One of the most devastating problems with poverty is that it limits or denies the poor the opportunity to be generous. Manipulating credit debts hardly enhances our dignity. Cajoling bill collectors is less than noble.

Human existence requires that we consume and that we take. We take from nature's bounty and the work of other persons. We are the recipients of an abundance of generosity from people we have never met or are even conscious of. But we do not have to give. Taking is a necessity, but giving is a choice. I submit that it is in giving that we experience our true freedom as human beings. We can choose what we give our money to and where we invest our time and energy. It is in our giving that we create and define our lives and the values that identify us.

Dr. Karl Menninger said, "Money giving is a symptom of a person's mental health. Generous people are seldom mentally ill." By sharing our substance, we give new life that will feed many people for years to come. It may be a library that will feed the mind or a museum that will feed the imagination or a church that will feed the soul of people, stirring them to justice and compassion.

William Ellery Channing wrote,

> How much may be done in this city to spread knowledge, vigor of thought, the sense of beauty, the pleasures of the imagination and the fine arts, and, above all, the influences of religion, through our whole community! Were the prosperous and educated to learn that, after providing for their families, they cannot better employ their possessions and influence than in forwarding the improvement and elevation of society, how soon would this city be regenerated.

Money is replete with many opportunities to create a better society. They are golden opportunities that will expand the vision of our fellow citizens, inviting them into a world of thought and beauty.

This is just the beginning of a long conversation. Money touches our self-esteem and our sense of security as families and as a church family. Money has tremendous influence on our personal success and our congregational success.

I hope that in this conversation, we will not feel ashamed or embarrassed or fearful. I hope we will not feel self-pitying or arrogant. I hope that we will appreciate the strengths and the limits of money in the life of our religious community. The church is not a business, but it does not have to be stupid in terms of financial management. May we be ever aware that the stewardship of our resources is a mark of maturity and wisdom. For out of the stewardship of our largess, our most important values are represented.

∾

Personal Reflection

Gary Blaine identifies many of the conflicts that money causes us, such as the guilt we feel over its importance to us and the fear and insecurity caused by poor management of our resources. What is the deepest conflict money or the use of money causes you? Even if you manage your money well and assume you do not have such conflicts, think carefully. Does your decision making revolve around finances more or less often than you would like it to? Does money, or the power it represents, play a role in your relationships? What would you like your descendants to say about how you used your resources?

For the Congregation

1. Make a list of the conflicts that money causes individuals, according to Gary Blaine's analysis. Can you add any to these? Now make a list of the conflicts that money causes congregations. Which of these are important in your congregation?

2. Based on your discussion of the previous question, which three
    conflicts on your list do you most need to address in your con-
    gregation? What changes would you like to see happen?

ALL THAT'S PAST IS PROLOGUE

REV. VICTORIA SAFFORD

White Bear Unitarian Universalist Church
Mahtomedi, Minnesota

This rich sermon weaves story and history, insight and challenge into a beautiful call to commit ourselves so that future Unitarian Universalists will inherit a worthy legacy. Victoria Safford's most immediate topic is planned giving, but her compelling theological underpinning is the connection between generosity and legacy.

Once we realize that it involves more than material resources, we can quickly see Safford's point that, intentionally or not, we all constantly leave legacies. We need to ask then, what kind of legacies do we want to give to those who come after us? "Planned giving," Safford says, "is about thinking of yourself already as an ancestor, a leaver of legacies for descendants you will never meet, but whose lives are already intertwined with yours." The cellist of Sarajevo who leaves the legacy of comfort and beauty, the woman on the train who provides the second glove so that the accidental recipient inherits a pair, the Unitarian Universalist who decides to contribute to a congregation's future so that a history of freedom and critical thinking will continue—all these people tap the generosity that results when we decide to become an active part of the future. Consider yourself as an ancestor. Start planning for your legacy. –S. M.

LAST YEAR FOR THE November Service Auction, a member of my congregation asked, and I agreed, to have a sermon topic listed among the many items available for bidding. Offering a sermon at auction is a tradition with which I am familiar, having done this before in another congregation, but because of that familiarity, I'm always a little wary. Why is it that the people most willing and able to bid high and win always choose topics like "Asphalt vs. Concrete" or "The Relevance of Post-Enlightenment Humanism for Religious Liberals and Secular Society on the Threshold of the 21st Century, Taking into Account Not Only the Classic Traditions of Jerusalem and Athens But Also Non-Western Ideologies Including But Not Limited to Buddhism, Jainism, Nine Centuries of Confucianism, and Late Twentieth-Century Wiccan Thought"? I really had to do that once, and everyone agreed that it was a dreadful Sunday morning.

This morning, though, the task is simpler—no less daunting but perhaps more interesting. Peter, who joined this church last year, was the successful bidder and has chosen as his theme "Planned Giving." He's interested in endowments and how churches establish them. He's interested in aggressive but socially responsible investing, not only in the market but in the future.

Planned giving is about standing on the solid ground of the present and leaning over time to touch the future. Planned giving is about coming of age. I know something, but not much, about this. Like this church, I began my life forty-something years ago on the cusp between the baby boomer generation and Generation X. Like this church and like some of you, I am now rounding the corner of what can only be called middle age, with what can only be called mixed feelings. And like the church, and like many of my peers, I had given little thought until recently to the long arc of my future as an older person. But now, as I turn that corner, I see that many of the things I thought I could change and influence, I maybe can't, while others, which I hadn't even seen before, beg for a shaping hand, a shove, a push, a pull, so they'll go in one direction and not some other. I begin to see that there are a few ways to affect the future, and now that I'm grown and even graying, I see that this would be the time to start.

Planned giving is about maturity. In congregations, it's about institutional maturity. As Peter has explained it to me, it's about rounding that corner and glimpsing a future that you, yourself, will not be part of but care passionately about anyway. Planned giving is about thinking of yourself already as an ancestor, a leaver of legacies for descendants whom you will never meet but whose lives are already intertwined with yours. We leave legacies, like it or not, on purpose or by accident: stories, values, traditions, toxic waste dumps, monuments, magnum opuses, mistakes, ethical ideals, rituals . . . and also, sometimes, money. (I think Peter was hoping that things would get specific here.) We leave cash, real estate, stock, and marketable securities. So herewith, a sermon on planned giving for Peter—an auction item, which, I might just mention, was sold more cheaply than the trout-fishing trip offered by my spouse. (Not that we were competing. Not that I was insulted.) A sermon about priorities.

This week, our attention is turned again toward the Balkans, toward what remains of and what might now become Yugoslavia. Amazing events are unfolding there, and I'm reminded of a person I read about some years ago, Vedran Smailovic, the cellist of Sarajevo. In the spring of 1992, one of the last bakeries still able to make bread in Sarajevo had a long line out the door as usual, stretching far into the street. At four o'clock in the afternoon, a shell hit directly into that bread line, and twenty-two people were instantly killed.

Vedran Smailovic lived nearby. Before the war, he had been the principal cellist of the Sarajevo Opera, and according to an article by Paul Sullivan in *Hope Magazine,*

> It was a distinguished and civilized life, and one to which he
> deeply and patiently longed to return. But when he saw the

carnage that day outside his window, he was pushed beyond his capacity to absorb and endure any more. He resolved to do the thing he could do best. . . . Every day thereafter, at 4:00 p.m., Vedran Smailovic put on his full, formal concert attire, took up his cello, and walked out of his apartment into the battle raging around him. He placed a little stool in the blood-stained, glass-splattered crater where the shell had landed, and every day, for twenty-two days, he played Albinoni's *Adagio* as tribute to the twenty-two dead. Snipers fired at him (they missed), mortar shells fell all around him, but he played that music to the abandoned streets, the smashed trucks, the burning buildings, and to the terrified people still hiding in the cellars, who heard him.

He played concerts elsewhere after that, including one in the middle of the ruins of the beautiful National Library. Now he lives in Belfast, Ireland, where he plays in Irish streets and Irish craters, and he also plays around the world. I heard him in a concert just before we moved and was surprised to see he is an ordinary person. He is an extraordinary cellist, but an ordinary person—long hair, cowboy boots, joking, friendly—a regular guy, not at all other-worldly, except for this way that he chooses to use up his life, to spend it. In Sarajevo he left a legacy, but in a strange container. This was no grand stage; no one even knew who he was at first. Since music is fleeting, the notes are heard only for a second, and only by a few, yet the power of the gesture carries on. This cellist is just an ordinary person, but his passion lingers; his courage, his defiance, his imagination, his playfulness, his art, his intention, all of these live on. The container for the legacy is memory, and when memory fades, when everyone who knows this story finally dies, it will become something else, part of a people's way of being, part of humanity's humanity. Such for us is immortality. It is probably significant that the cellist of Sarajevo grew up in a distinguished family of musicians. His father, a famous violin-

ist, founded a family ensemble called *Musica ad Hominem*—
Music for the People—and he brought his children, including
young Vedran, to play in poor villages and neighborhoods all over
Yugoslavia, bringing live classical music to people who otherwise
would hear none. His father's generosity of spirit lives on. "All
that's past is prologue" as Shakespeare writes; what's happened in
the past, what happens in the present, has bearing on the future.

And this reminds me of our own "people's music" here this
morning, this folk tradition carried on and passed along, another
kind of *musica ad hominem*. And of course a large portion of the
American folk tradition is just outright fun, plain and simple, but
a larger portion is about hope, fear, solidarity, justice, peace,
oppression, slavery, dignity, faith and freedom, freedom, freedom.

In an interview once, Smailovic said, "I worry. I am afraid. Are
you? It is not enough just to pray, to whatever God, for a better
future. It is necessary that we take urgent, healthy action to return
ourselves to the beauty of a life without fear." Healthy, urgent
action—creative, generous action—restores our lives to beauty,
even if, and perhaps especially if, that action involves risk, at least
the risk of never knowing if your action is the right one, or
whether it will matter, or how things will turn out.

Ours is a movement that, from its first beginnings, has survived and thrived on the edge of risk. For over three hundred
years in this country, and much longer in Europe, Unitarian
Universalism has been part of a liberal religious tradition that, to
some extent, defines itself in terms of risk, living on the edge, the
frontier, the fringe. In its earliest incarnation as the far left wing
of the radical Reformation, our movement involved dissent from
the Roman Church, the Lutheran Church, and the Church of
Calvin, and following its truth meant risking your life. It meant
the risk of imprisonment or exile or burning at the stake, the risk
of becoming one of our martyrs, whose hymns we still sing and
whose writings we still read for clues about our own humanity.
From those early generations of religious freedom fighters to

these later times, when seekers come to our congregations leaving the traditions of their childhood and all the pain and struggle that implies, ours has been an enterprise involving risk. Being here, I like to think, involves healthy, urgent action to restore ourselves to the beauty of a life without fear.

Ours is a saving church, and by that I mean that lives are saved within it. People still say that; they use that old vocabulary. They say, "I never knew there was a place like this, where I could be accepted." They say, "I never knew there could be a congregation that believed as I do." They say, "I walked out of the church as soon as I was old enough, but until I came here, I had no idea how deeply I was longing for connection to other people and also to the sacred." They say, "I was a spiritual shipwreck, and I'm still drifting, but at least, at last, I have a home." For me, it was astonishing to discover this tradition. I was a young adult, flailing around at large out there, and when I accidentally stumbled upon the works of William Ellery Channing one rainy afternoon, a door opened to me. Here was someone in print, someone who wrote in 1819, asking the unspeakable questions I'd been asking, doubting the "truths" that I'd been doubting, clearly defining the moral ideas, the theological ideas that I had harbored all along as crazy. Here was a religion welcoming science and reason while honoring mystery and wonder. Here was a religion concerned more with deeds than creeds, a church that in its Sunday Schools apparently taught children to think and act and feel—to know their hearts instead of to recite. I felt not as if my soul were saved but as if my self were somehow integrated, my integrity restored, as if mind and heart and soul were reunited after a long, strange, unnatural parting of the ways.

Ours is a saving church, and it is a church that acts. This week, one of you brought in a flyer about a march and vigil to be held on racial profiling and violence, what some in the neighborhoods there are calling the crime of "driving while black." Does this concern us, this inner city, urban issue? Does this concern us way out in the whiter wilderness of our town? It absolutely does, and we will be there. Last week, I heard, from a parent, news of a deeply disturbing homophobic incident that occurred in a high school in a town not far from here. Though the call to respond went out to many, members of this congregation are the ones who have actually come forward, adults and youth, to speak out and offer resources and see what healthy, urgent action they might be called to take. One parent, when asked whether his work on gay rights in the school might be hard to explain to his middle school child, responded, "Yes, it will be. We haven't talked about this stuff before. But it would be harder to explain to her later if I just did nothing."

This is a saving church and a church that acts. It is also a church that asks and wonders, unafraid of questions that may go unanswered, unafraid of answers that may challenge its assumptions. In Channing's words, it will not "content itself with a passive or hereditary faith, but opens itself to light whencesoever it may come. It does not mechanically copy the past, but listens for new and higher monitions of conscience." This is a church that asks how it might possibly continue to be relevant, so that when Nicholas, the baby who was dedicated this morning, comes of age, he might wish to be a part of it. This is a church that asks how it can serve that baby well, today while he is a child and right on into his old age, which none of us will be there to see. How will we encourage his unspeakable questions, how will we nurture his sense of justice, his love of freedom, his faith, his spirit, and most of all, his hope? What songs will we teach him to sing? What prayers will we offer from our own hearts as examples? This is a saving church, a church that acts and a church that asks. These are some of the reasons why some of us are part of it and why we contribute to its thriving in whatever ways we can.

How do you make a legacy? What kind of healthy, urgent action in the present has any bearing on the future?

My colleague, Jane Rzepka, tells a story about a woman on a subway train in New York City: The station was crowded, and as she left the train she realized she was holding only one of her gloves. She looked back into the car and saw the matching one on the seat, but it was too late to rush back and retrieve it. Suddenly, as the doors began to close, she flung out her arm and tossed the remaining glove onto the seat alongside its mate. The doors shut, and the train pulled away.

That looks like a frivolous gesture, gratuitous, spontaneous, spur of the moment. But you know she must have lived a long life of generosity, a life of wild and creative generosity of spirit, to be able to think so quickly, to act so urgently and healthily, to know precisely in that moment what would bless the world right then and there. It happened in an instant, but that was planned giving, through and through. Something in her past, or everything in her past, prepared her for her gesture—habits of living and giving practiced and refined her whole life-long. All our past is prologue, and it prepares us for these opportunities.

How do you make a legacy? Some people play the cello in extraordinary venues. Others risk their lives, their selves, their souls in congregations, struggling against the odds to be who they are and who they are called to be. Some toss the other glove, deliberately and gladly and regularly, with no regrets. All this is planned giving; it does not occur by accident, however spontaneous it looks. These acts are intentional. They require effort and choices about spending. How will you spend, or use up, your life? Some who have it give their time or their money, mindful that these substances, like musical notes, are fleeting; you bless these gifts by the use you put them to.

Last year here, when this congregation sustained a hard succession of losses—the deaths of several beloved members all in a row—people made contributions in their honor before we even had an endowment vehicle in place. They sent gifts and enclosed notes saying, in one way or another, "Please make this money a memorial to that person's life so that all she gave us might continue and blossom and thrive for people who will never know her or me. Please make this money a memorial, an inheritance for future members of this congregation and the causes they will someday serve." They didn't mean, "Balance out the budget with my check," or "Buy paper clips and pay the bills and pay the staff and let that be that." They meant, "Let these funds be a gift from the ancestors to the descendants. Out of our grieving and our gratitude, let this gift live on." That is planned giving, planned living—placing one's self in the camp of the ancestors and imagining the descendants.

Some can give time or money. Some teach their children old and simple songs and not so simple struggles—the *Musica ad Hominem* that's sung in every language—so that when new struggles come along, those children will have something to fall back on, a tradition of freedom and justice. Some support the congregation they believe in, and the congregation that believes in them, simply with their presence, which is all they can give, which is enough, and which, in and of itself, makes the place a holy place.

And somewhere this morning, there is a child, perhaps in Sarajevo, perhaps in Belgrade, maybe in a far-off place to which she was brought as a refugee. She is ten now, or eleven, or maybe twelve, and in her mind she is remembering a phrase of sad and wondrous music that she heard when she was very small and very scared. And she is wondering how she's going to learn to play the cello, how she will take lessons, because this gift was given to her, on purpose, with intention, by a man she doesn't know, who received it from his father who received it from someone long ago. They passed it on as she will pass it on, and all of this, by their love and their integrity, was and will be planned. There is no such thing as unplanned giving.

James Baldwin, African-American philosopher and novelist, wrote,

It is rare indeed that people give.
Most people guard and keep;
they suppose that it is they themselves and what they

identify with themselves that they are guarding and
  keeping,
whereas what they are actually guarding and keeping is
  their system of reality and what they assume themselves to be.
One can give nothing whatever without giving oneself—
  that is to say, risking oneself.
If one cannot risk oneself,
then one is simply incapable of giving.

~

Personal Reflection

Much of the time, we do not like to think about the future of
which we will not be a part. One of the most telling points
Victoria Safford makes, though, is that we leave legacies, intentionally or not, just by virtue of having lived. And it is through
those legacies that we do belong to the world of the future. With
the beautiful story of the cellist, she suggests how important it is
to leave an intentional legacy. What are the legacies you are creating, intentional or otherwise? If you could plan the giving to be
done in the next stage of your life, what would you like it to be?

For the Congregation

1. In your congregation, how do you teach your children the
    musica ad hominem, the traditions and songs and stories they
    can fall back on in their own struggles for justice? Does it
    happen in religious education? What are the less obvious
    ways in which this important inspiration is passed along?
2. To engage in planned giving and planned living, says Victoria
    Safford, we must put ourselves in the place of ancestors and
    imagine our descendants. If you think of the congregation
    which will inherit your legacy twenty-five, fifty, or seventy-

five years from now, what would you like its members to say about the gift that you collectively gave?

3. What are the three major obstacles you face in planning financially for your congregation's future? Why do these challenge you? What positive steps can you take to overcome these obstacles?

WHO WANTS TO BE A MILLIONAIRE?

REV. GARY KOWALSKI

The First Unitarian Universalist Society
Burlington, Vermont

Gary Kowalski raises a question with important implications, not only for our stewardship but for our spiritual well-being. Does wealth, he asks, "consist in how much we are able to accumulate and possess, or is wealth better measured by how much we feel we can afford to share?" Persons with great wealth who focus on hoarding and accumulating even more are rarely either generous or spiritually whole.

Nothing else in life can provide the satisfaction and meaning that come from working with others toward a common goal and working in the service of our most deeply held values. Although we do not always connect sacrifice and generosity in our minds, they are clearly two sides of the same coin. Our religious communities offer us unique opportunity to work with kindred souls to perpetuate the values we most cherish. In the process, our sacrifice brings us spiritual wealth.

Consider investing in your dreams, Kowalski says. I hope that's just what you will want to do after reading this sermon. –S. M.

FANTASIES SOMETIMES reveal undisclosed information about ourselves: our hidden phobias, unspoken desires, and unexamined
motives. And group fantasies say much about our culture—our
society's real values as opposed to the ideals that receive mainly lip
service.

Maybe that's why I find myself occasionally watching the
popular TV quiz show, *Who Wants to Be a Millionaire?* Partly, I
tune in for the same reason eighteen million other viewers do so.
I like to match my wits against the contestants to see if I can
answer the tough questions like "What is the capitol of Australia?"
(I'll give you a hint: It's not Sydney or Melbourne) and to groan
when players miss the easy ones. ("In the title of a 1950s Chuck
Berry song, what classical composer is asked to 'roll over'?") The
questions are harder than you expect, but not impossibly hard, so
that any one of us might imagine ourselves sitting in the contes-
tant's seat listening to Regis ask, "Is that your final answer?" and
wondering whether we have what it takes to win a million bucks.
And who hasn't, at one time or another, entertained a fantasy of
instant wealth and riches?

But while I can enjoy the show on one level, I find myself
troubled by it on another. What accounts for the fantastically high
ratings the program receives? Why has it spun off a host of imita-
tors, from *Greed* to *Who Wants to Marry a Multimillionaire?*, all of
which feature the drawing card of quick money with no real
expenditure of effort? How is it that so many Americans' fondest
dream seems to be winning the lottery? Why has gambling
become a national obsession so that people now spend more
money in casinos than they do on all other forms of entertainment, including sports, movies, and the music industry combined? What accounts for the explosive growth of day-trading in
the stock market except that hordes of people think they can
make a quick dollar without any of the patience or self-discipline
required of more traditional investors? The phenomenal popular-
ity of *Who Wants to Be a Millionaire?* seems to be based on the fact

that it has struck a nerve. Its Nielsens have rocketed because so many people have begun to lose the ability to distinguish between fantasy and reality. More and more seem to believe that the good life is within easy reach—the *good life* being defined solely in material terms, and the way to get there being mostly a matter of luck and timing rather than hard work and perseverance. That truly is a delusion.

Now there may be a grain of truth there somewhere. I don't want to say that money is not important or that the fickle finger of fate doesn't play a role in determining who gets rich and who doesn't. When asked to share his own personal formula for success, J. Paul Getty gave the advice to get up early, work hard, and strike oil. There are racial disparities in the distribution of wealth that need to be addressed, and men still earn more than women for doing the same jobs. But to a surprising extent, the people who wind up wealthy in America do so not because they happen to be born white or male or with a silver spoon in their mouths and not because they happen to know who invented Velcro or sang back-up for the Supremes. When you look at the social and economic statistics, you find that most of the people who really are millionaires have some very simple things in common:

> They save their money and invest it over time.
> They don't have flashy lifestyles or buy expensive clothes or luxury cars.
> Most of them went to public schools, not prep schools or private academies.
> Most never inherited a dime from their parents.
> And most expect to work hard, somewhere between forty-five and fifty-five hours per week.

These are all among the findings of Thomas Stanley and William Danko, from their book *The Millionaire Next Door*, which examines the question of who really has money in the United States. They dispel the illusion that millionaires live more extravagantly than the rest of us. Most live far more frugally than their middle-class neighbors. And the authors turn up some surprising data regarding ethnicity. You might not guess that Turks or Palestinians are more than twice as likely to have a million dollars as the average American household or that Americans of Russian descent have a better chance at hitting the jackpot than White Anglo-Saxon Protestants. But that's what the numbers show. Many millionaires are first-generation immigrants to this country. It's their children and grandchildren—the second and third generations—who are more likely to fritter the money away as they become acculturated into a shop-till-you-drop society.

You might ask the question, then: Can anybody get rich, if they work hard, live simply, save, and invest? I'm not sure I'd go that far. But that would seem to be the implication if you consider the life of Oseola McCarty of Hattiesburg, Mississippi, who made headlines in 1995 when she donated $150,000 to start a scholarship fund for African-American students in financial need. Ms. McCarty, who passed away last year, was eighty-eight years old when she signed a charitable trust, transferring her wealth to the state university at the time of her death. She started work in the sixth grade when she had to drop out of school to take care of a sick aunt and spent the next seventy-five years taking in other people's laundry, starting out at $1.50 a bundle. Ms. McCarty, who never owned a car and was in the habit of walking wherever she needed to go, noted, "The secret to building a fortune is compounding interest. It's not the ones that make the big money, but the ones who know how to save who get ahead." She recalls, "I started saving when I was a little girl, just to have candy money. When I got grown, I started saving for my future. I'd go to the bank once a month, hold out just enough to cover my expenses, and put the rest into my savings account. Every month, I'd save the same and put it away. I was consistent." Later, she began putting money into mutual funds and CDs. But it was the consistency that paid off. And her generosity inspired matching gifts that tripled the size of her bequest, creating a scholarship fund of almost half a million dollars, directly inspiring media mogul Ted Turner to donate one billion dollars to the United Nations. Some of McCarty's tips for getting rich?

> I don't like to waste. I keep everything—clothes, furniture, housewares—until it wears out. Usefulness often outlasts style.
>
> I don't buy clothes very often, but when I do, I try to find something on sale. I'll spend a little more for something of higher quality if I have the money to spare.
>
> I think a Christmas savings account is a good idea. Every year, I save and prepare to spend that money. It's crazy the way some people will get into debt at that time of the year.
>
> Credit cards are okay for some people, but I wouldn't go for one. I try not to spend money that I don't have, buying what I can't afford.

Of course, Ms. McCarty also needed a reason to save. Part of her reason was self-interested. "A smart person plans for the future," she said. "You never know what kind of emergency will come up and can't rely on the government to meet all your needs. You have to take responsibility for yourself." Part of the reason she was such a good steward of her money was altruistic however: She wanted to give other people opportunities that she never had. "I can't do everything," she observed. "But I can do something to help somebody. And what I can do, I will do. I wish I could do more."

I wonder how many of us are as rich as Osceola McCarty? Rich not only in monetary terms but also in spiritual terms. It raises the question of how we define wealth. Does it consist of how much we are able to accumulate and possess, or is wealth better measured by how much we feel we can afford to share? I suspect that many of us struggle with the tension between the desire to do well and the desire to do good. Part of what we want from life is comfort, security, and independence, but another important part of what we want is the satisfaction that comes from sharing values, working together in a common cause, and belonging to something larger and more lasting than ourselves.

Two university professors who recently released the results of an investigation into what makes people happy found (not surprisingly) that money was an important indicator in determining whether people described themselves as very happy, somewhat happy, or fairly unhappy. But money was not nearly as significant as other factors, like having a good marriage, and was only one among an assortment of other predictors, including being part of a meaningful religious community.

Now, being part of a religious community, like being part of a good marriage, demands a special set of attitudes and expectations on the part of the participants. If we approach the relationship with a mentality of "What's in it for me?" we are almost certainly setting ourselves up for disappointment and failure. But unfortunately, that attitude is all too common in our cash-and-carry society. People frequently come through the doors of our meetinghouse bringing with them the mindset of the marketplace, as church shoppers or consumers. They evaluate their experience on Sunday morning by the same criteria they might use to judge the worth of other, competing attractions. And what they give to support the congregation is based on what they might expect to pay for similar services from seemingly similar retailers. If a cup of coffee costs a dollar at Starbucks, they figure, it may be worth a dollar to have coffee at the social hour following the service. If babysitting averages five dollars an hour, they reason that a ten-dollar bill in the collection plate should cover the costs of bringing one child to church school with another in the nursery. And from one point of view, that's a good way to calculate the value of what you get from a congregation. But people who come to Unitarian Universalism seeking spiritual goods are likely to be disappointed so long as they have the outlook of consumers in search of material goods. If their connection to our liberal faith is to grow into something more rewarding, they have to give up the consumer mind set and begin to think of themselves instead as shareholders, investors, co-owners in what happens in church, just as the parties in a marriage see themselves as partners rather than competitors with a joint share in the success of the enterprise. Making the transition from consumer to investor involves an emotional shift, but also a financial one. At that point, what people pledge to support their religious community is likely to increase significantly, but the profit, the payback, the dividends also rise dramatically.

Many years ago, Mohandas Gandhi made a list of what he called the seven sins of the modern world. High on the list were these two: wealth without work and religion without sacrifice. I tend to agree with Gandhi. I think we do suffer from the delusion that we can get something for nothing. I think our get-rich-quick economy tends to denigrate the value of struggle, commitment, and sacrifice. Maybe I'm old-fashioned, but I agree with Osceola McCarty, who said, "hard work gives life meaning. Everyone needs to work hard at something to feel good about themselves. Every job can be done well and every day has its satisfactions."

TV game shows may promise you instant wealth as the key to happiness. But I don't really believe that promise. The question for me is: What can we promise to one another? And I think the answer is that we can promise each other hard, honest work— the work of raising caring children in an often uncaring world, the work of trying to live with integrity in a world rife with sham and deception, the work of building a community where each person has dignity because of who they are, not because of what they earn or how much they own.

Imagining that you're going to win the lottery, or that it would solve all your problems even if you did, really is farfetched. Winning the sweepstakes is a one-in-ten-million chance. Marrying a multimillionaire may be what producers call "reality-based" programming, but it's TV reality. It doesn't apply to you or me. But it's not farfetched at all to believe that everybody—each one of us—can have a life that means something, that's rich in love, and that makes a difference. So what I'm inviting you to do is not to buy into a fantasy but to consider investing in a dream.

~

Personal Reflection

Gary Kowalski makes it abundantly clear that we can be rich in many ways besides simple material wealth. Where does your greatest wealth lie? Do you give it away as generously as you would like and toward an end in which you believe?

For the Congregation

1. Does your congregation ever indulge in get-rich-quick fantasies? Explain. Could it have negative effects on a congregation to get rich quickly?

2. What is the hard work needed to pay for your congregation's dreams?

3. As Gary Kowalski points out, Gandhi said two of the sins of the modern world are wealth without work and religion without sacrifice. What sacrifices does your congregation call on you to make? What makes that sacrifice worthwhile?

GOING IT ALONE

REV. DAVID R. WEISSBARD

Unitarian Universalist Church
Rockford, Illinois

This sermon confronts the question most Unitarian Universalists eventually ask: "What do we get from being a part of the Unitarian Universalist Association?" David Weissbard offers the bold statement that our congregations should either take seriously the need to support the Association by paying their Fair Share or cut their ties. One by one, he names objections to supporting the Association and then suggests what congregational life would be like without the ties that bind.

The sermon is rich in weaving contemporary Unitarian Universalist practice with Unitarian and Universalist history. The two work together to create the fabric of what we experience as Unitarian Universalism, a reality the author more implies than states. But his meaning is clear.

Weissbard points out the importance most Unitarian Universalists place on their home congregations. In most people's eyes, we simply could not "go it alone" as individuals. Many of the benefits members receive from a congregation result from membership in the Association. There is a symmetry to life that we do not always see. —S. M.

THE SCHEDULE in our house has worked like this. Karen wakes up at 5:00, and I generally get up at 5:30 or 6:00. Karen leaves for work at 6:30. I am often on the computer in the morning. The way it was going, Hilary, our seven-year-old, would call down to me at 8:00 or so when she woke up, and I would take her a bowl of Cheerios, which she'd eat on a bed table while she watched kids' shows on television. At 8:20 or so, I'd start nagging her to get dressed, which took about twenty minutes. Since her bus comes at 8:42, those last twenty minutes were frantic, and we sometimes got mad at each other.

Finally, I had a brainstorm. "Let's get out of this pattern," I said. "From now on, Hilary will get her clothes on first and then eat." Doing her own part to break the pattern, she informed me that she no longer liked Cheerios, so we got a disgusting new cereal. The tension is gone; the new approach is working like a charm.

In fact, the other day, I fell back asleep reading the paper and didn't get Hilary up until 8:10. I told her to get dressed, and I turned on the TV as I went to get her cereal. She said, "Dad, I don't get dressed well while the TV is on."

The breakthrough came when I realized that we were locked in a pattern that was not paying off. That happens in organizations, too. We certainly do it in church.

Problems Needing Creative Solutions

When I thought about counterproductive patterns into which we have locked ourselves, I thought about my ongoing frustration regarding our congregation's support, or non-support, of the Association of Congregations of which we are a part. Each year at budget time, I advocate meeting our responsibility to the Unitarian Universalist Association by paying the full-share contribution, which is, in fact, paid by two out of every three other congregations. Usually, this amount goes into the preliminary budget, but it comes out of the final budget when we find we "can't afford it." Every time, I get a burning sensation in my stomach.

If we were to step back and look creatively at how to change this, we could not avoid asking the fundamental question, "Do we really need the Association? Why not go it alone?"

An Historical Reminder

A two-minute historical orientation to religious liberalism in Rockford is in order. A Unitarian congregation and a Universalist congregation were founded in Rockford in 1841. The Universalists joined with the Unitarians soon after. It was a somewhat fractious group, calling ministers and then sending them packing when there wasn't enough money to pay them. One student of our history suggested that it was because the Universalists were more conservative and quickly became dissatisfied with the liberal Unitarian ministers called by the majority. In June of 1870, the Reverend D. M. Reed, then minister, resigned during a statistically healthy period, allegedly because of poor health, although he lived another twenty years. Before the church had an opportunity to seek a new minister, the very liberal Baptist minister, Dr. Thomas Kerr, resigned his pulpit, and in September 1870, forty-eight members of the First Baptist Church who resigned with Dr. Kerr joined with members of the United Unitarian Universalist Church to form a new liberal non-denominational church that they called The Church of the Christian Union.

The theoretically non-denominational church was, in fact, closely aligned with the Unitarian movement. When the cornerstone of its new building was laid in 1888, virtually all of the guest speakers were Unitarians, and a great Unitarian hymn writer wrote a special hymn for the event. Dr. Kerr received associate fellowship as a Unitarian minister. Unitarian hymnbooks and Unitarian Sunday School curricula were used in the church. But it was a non-denominational church, so it had no obligation and contributed no money to the American Unitarian Association. I can find no indication of how the congregation found the Reverend Robert Bryant, the successor to Dr. Kerr, but it is clear in the records that the secretary of the Western Unitarian Conference helped put the church in touch with the Reverend Thornton Anthony Mills, Bryant's successor, and the church did send a small contribution to that group. The next minister, Dr. Charles Parker Connolly, who was called in 1913, was a Congregationalist in background, but he quickly became involved in Unitarian circles. In 1928 the congregation voted to affiliate formally with the American Unitarian Association, which merged with the Universalist Church of America in 1961 to become the Unitarian Universalist Association.

The UUA

The UUA is an association of independent congregations. Its primary purpose, according to its bylaws, is "to serve the needs of its member congregations, organize new congregations, extend and strengthen Unitarian Universalist institutions and implement its principles." The support of the Association, like the support of our own church, is entirely voluntary. As with our church, there is a requirement that members contribute, but the amount is not specified. In practice, the Association's Board annually designates an amount which is a "suggested share" based on so much per member. (The current amount is $39 per member.) The reality is that most of our churches and fellowships take that number seriously, and more than two-thirds of them give at least that amount, while some give more. It has been many years since the Rockford church has come even close to giving its full share, $19,000, and it is currently giving $10,000.

When I have raised the issue of this discrepancy, some people have insisted that the UUA isn't worth that much to us. Others have urged full support only until we come to the point at which we would have to cut something local to meet our continental responsibility. It may be important, but it's not that important.

Hence my radical suggestion: How about our "going it alone"? Since we are not prepared to be a fully responsible mem-

ber of the Association, perhaps we should sever our ties and go
back to our former status of sympathetic but unaffiliated. We
could save $10,000 and any guilt we might carry about being only
partly responsible. (And Ralph Waldo Emerson suggested a minister would not dare to examine "the ground of his institution.")

What's It Worth?

A reasonable question to ask is, "What do we get from being a part
of the UUA?"

The reason for the founding of the American Unitarian
Association in 1825, according to William Ellery Channing, was
"to spread our views of religion; not our mere opinions, for our
religion is essentially practical. The convention should bring
together [people] from every part of the country to compare their
views, and ascertain the wants of different places."

Fundamentally, the job of the gathered group was to print
pamphlets and support growth of new churches in the West (i. e.,
West of Worcester). The UUA continues to print pamphlets that
we use to introduce ourselves to visitors, and it supports the
growth of new churches. But we could probably print our own
pamphlets, and, we ask, does a new church in Door County,
Wisconsin, really affect us?

Religious Education

It is true that we would be hard-pressed (impossibly pressed) to
do religious education without the curricula that are written,
field-tested, and published for us by the UUA. It is not very pro-
ductive to throw kids and a teacher in a classroom and say, "Be
together." The being together is important, but it is fostered by the
curricula that we choose as a context for that interaction, and we
do have values to share and support. Most of what happens in our
church school is a result of UUA published curricula. Now, some
have suggested that since most of our members have grown up in
traditional Christian churches, maybe it would be more effective

to close our church school and ship our kids off to a Christian church against which they can later rebel. And then there are also the adult education materials that the Association develops. One possibility, of course, is simply to buy curricula from the UUA at its publication cost, which is a very small portion of the actual cost. Morally, we'd be stealing, but hey, what the heck!

Ministry

Perhaps next in line of importance is ministry. The UUA helps to recruit students for the ministry and to support seminary education, albeit to an inadequate degree. It then, as we know from some dissatisfaction with the process, tries to filter from that graduating pool people whom it believes are not prepared to offer the quality of ministerial leadership expected by our congregations. There are goofs in both directions—passing some they should not and placing obstacles in front of some who should be encouraged. Probably the most essential service in the eyes of many is the intensive process for helping to match prospective ministers with congregations in search. Now, some of our members have pointed out that we could save a lot of money by seeking out a liberal Methodist instead of a UU minister; their ministers are paid a lot less than ours. Or, if we disaffiliated with the UUA, our church could simply pirate ministers who had been educated with UU scholarship money and gained experience in UU congregations. I know of one liberal Baptist church that does that, but it has succeeded by offering salaries that even UUs can't turn down. There go the savings, and that isn't really ethical conduct.

Other Services

The UUA also provides congregations with consultant services, like the canvass consultant who helped us so much two years ago at a price much lower than we would have paid on the open market, as well as consultants in conflict resolution, religious education, capital fund drives, social justice, and church growth. There are interfaith organizations from which we could purchase these services as long as we are prepared to do the theological and structural translating that is necessary; they often don't understand our form of governance.

The UUA Faith in Action Department keeps us in touch with ways in which we can speak out in the world for the principles we value. That department initiated the Welcoming Congregation program and has stood out nationally in issues of gay, lesbian, bisexual and transgender people's rights. It is that office that helps us address issues like abortion, gun control, privacy, racial justice, and religious freedom beyond our local community. But maybe the American Civil Liberties Union, the League of Women Voters, and Rockford Peace and Justice suffice. Do we really need that service from Boston?

The UUA that, through a major process, developed our new hymnals, as it and its predecessor organizations did the earlier versions. One local church could never do that, but then again, we have members who would be just as happy to sing the old Christian hymns or no hymns at all. Then there are the international and interfaith activities in which the Association represents us, but if we became simply the Liberal Church of Rockford, we wouldn't need any of that stuff.

Ditto for the *World* magazine, which keeps our members informed about what UUs are doing around the country and world. And there are the annual General Assemblies, which offer a tremendous, diverse, and intense experience of Unitarian Universalism, but few of our members ever attend those. There is a variety of electronic communication going on now, with many specialized groups sharing programs and ideas over the Internet, and there is the UUA homepage, which offers information that is tapped into quite frequently. But none of that is really important to us, is it? The truth is, a lot of what any organization does is aimed at self-preservation and self-enhancement. There are times when it seems as if the people at our headquarters in Boston act as if it is the headquarters that is most important and the reason for local churches like ours to survive is simply to support the existence of the headquarters staff.

The Central Reason

The hardest to pin down but probably the most important reason for our affiliation with the UUA is that it makes us more than an isolated congregation in Rockford, Illinois. By being part of the Association, we link ourselves with two historical movements dating back two millennia, and with a small, but hopefully effective, contemporary liberal religious movement with 150,000 adult members. Would it be the same if we were to become the Liberal Church of Rockford and sever that connection? If we are honest, that local presence is all that matters on any practical level for many of our members. Few of our adult members come into contact with UUs out of town; their concern is primarily local.

We Could Go It Alone

In all honesty, I have to tell you that our church could survive without the larger Unitarian Universalist movement, at least for a while. We've done it before, and we could do it again. There would be some losses, but maybe there would be some gains. It is clear that, unlike those other religions which are legitimized by their connection to a central authority structure that has a measure of control over them, we do not need a continental organization to make us a valid church.

The Church?

If we are really going to get down to the nitty-gritty and examine the ground of the institution, this line of reasoning forces us to raise the even larger question of the need for any church at all. Our church does not offer its members any keys to the Kingdom of God. No supernatural blessing is carried by participation in our church. There is an old saying that you can really be a

Unitarian Universalist by yourself.

Virtually everything the church can offer is available somewhere else. There is intellectual stimulation available from a variety of sources. There are gurus like Brother Macki and others who
come to town periodically or are available on tape or television.
There are organizations for social justice.

There are other sources of counseling. Take it apart piece by
piece, and you can get it all somewhere else. What if we were to
sell our building to our neighbors at Rockford College and use
the proceeds for housing the poor or reducing the school deficit
or some other good cause? What if the $350,000 it takes a year
to operate our church were channeled directly into other good
causes? If you can be a Unitarian Universalist by yourself, then
seriously, who really needs the church?

Putting It Back Together

As a kid, I was really good at taking things apart, but not so good
at putting them back together. I hope I can do better this evening,
or we are in big trouble.

Independence vs. Interdependence

The reading from Emerson's *Self-Reliance* speaks of our belief in
the virtue of "going it alone." That is an important part of our
cultural heritage, particularly the liberal heritage. Remember
Emerson's words: "It is only as a man puts off all foreign support
and stands alone, that I see him to be strong and to prevail." What
did Emerson prefer in a church? The silent church with people
sitting around in utter privacy as if they had walls around them,
which, in New England box pews, they did.

Traditionally, Unitarian Universalist churches attract people
who are independent, people who are not looking for a religion in
which they are dependent on a supernatural power or an author-
itarian structure. People who want those things do not stick
around long. I have come to believe that self-reliance lives in a

healthy tension with community. Our individual integrity is important, but so is cooperation. One of the great concerns of our time is what is being called *the new communitarianism*—a realization of the need among people for community.

Voluntary Associations

The great Unitarian leader William Ellery Channing envisioned this modern concern for community 170 years ago. Channing is seen by some as one of the original articulators of the importance of voluntary associations. Writing in 1829, Channing said,

> People, if it is justly said, can do jointly what they cannot do singly. The union of minds and hands works wonders. [People] grow efficient by concentrating their powers. Joint effort conquers nature, hews through mountains, rears pyramids, dikes out of the ocean. [People] left to [themselves] living without [others], if [they] could indeed so live, would be one of the weakest of creatures. Associated with [their] kind, [they] gain dominion over the strongest animals, over the earth and the sea...

Nor is this all:

> [People] not only accumulate power by union, but gain warmth and earnestness. The heart is kindled. An electric communication is established between those who are brought nigh and bound to each other, in common labors. [People] droop in solitude. No sound excites us like the voice of a fellow-creature. The mere sight of a human countenance, brightened with strong and generous emotion, gives new strength to act or suffer.

Channing was fully aware of the dangers of associations dominating individuals—all the sins that concerned Emerson—but it was his belief that if we were cautious, the potential good of people voluntarily linking themselves to others was worth the risk.

The Church

If you accept the value of cooperation and community as being of at least equal importance with self-reliance, let us look again at the church. I disavow none of what I said earlier. The pieces of what the church offers are all available elsewhere. What the church offers uniquely is the combination of all of them in a community gathered around certain principles.

Why is it that so many of our members say that life in Rockford would, for them, be unthinkable without our church?

The word *Unitarian* historically referred to the unity rather than to the three-personed view of deity. In a modern sense, it can be seen as a testimony to the unity of our lives. Our churches are places where we gather to celebrate our joys and concerns, articulate our dreams, and acknowledge our disappointments. Our churches are places where we gather in a community that began before us and that we are committed to helping continue after us.

There is much in our lives that is transient, but for many of our members, this church represents a long-term commitment. Some are here only for as long as it "feels good," as long as it is meeting their needs. Such members come and go through the traditional revolving door. But our church is really about those who sink their roots in it, who stand with it through good times and bad, who declare that it is their church, come what may, because they feel empowered by their relationship to it. They are the church.

The Larger Movement

That brings us back to the question with which we began, with the value of our larger movement, the Unitarian Universalists beyond our communities. I would suggest to you that the non-denominational independent Church of the Christian Union was, in a sense, a fraud. It could not have been what it was without its connections to the Unitarian movement. It was, to be brutally honest, a kind of parasite, living off something without contributing to it in return.

Just as we are in our churches because we need one another and gain strength from being together, so too our individual churches need the support of their sister churches, and they gain strength from being part of a larger movement that makes us more significant than we would be alone. More important than anything the UUA does is the fact that it is. An excess of self-reliance is our version of original sin—it is our curse. We alone are not enough.

But if we are to be a part of the larger church, we need to fully accept not only the benefits but the responsibilities of membership. We need to affirm our commitment to support it in a way that is consistent with other congregations, and stop treating our local needs and desires as the overwhelming concern, letting the UUA take the hindmost. We are troubled that some of our members treat us that way. We should be troubled when we treat the UUA that way.

We cannot just go it alone. We need others. We need other individuals, which is why we have our churches. Our churches need the support of other congregations, which is why we have an Association of congregations. As our local congregations sustain us, so our Association sustains the local congregations. We always have the option of going it alone, but we need not to pretend that we are doing so when it comes to our responsibilities and claim otherwise when we collect the benefits of our ties.

We need to be responsible in our relationships. We need to decide consciously what relationship we want to have with our larger movement. If, in fact, it is not important enough to us to support it fully, then the most honorable path would be to cut ourselves off from it altogether. I urge you to give serious consideration to that relationship and to how we will respond to the responsibilities it places on us.

~

Personal Reflection

When in your life have you tried to go it alone? What was the experience like? How is this different than times when you have struggled for a cause or toward a goal with the support of others?

For the Congregation

1. How is David Weissbard's opening story about his family life related to the topic of whether a congregation needs the Unitarian Universalist Association? What point is he making?
2. While he is saying his congregation could go it alone, Weissbard is obviously making the opposite case. List the major functions the UUA serves. How do these apply to your congregation?
3. Are there times when your congregation has tried to go it alone? How did that affect the life of the congregation?
4. Do the members of your congregation ever present these arguments about supporting the Association? If so, how might you engage the congregation in dialogue about these issues?

LEARN TO FLY

REV. AMANDA L. AIKMAN

Evergreen Unitarian Universalist Fellowship
Marysville, Washington

*Flying is perhaps the most archetypal metaphor for freedom; it even
occurs in our dreams. So it is that Amanda Aikman uses a metaphor
of learning to fly in her racquetball game to invite us into consider-
ing what a congregation can mean to us. "Institution," Aikman says,
"is not a very thrilling word." No surprise there, not for Unitarian
Universalists anyway. But her next statement catches us off guard:
"What it means to me is freedom. The freedom not to have to keep
re-inventing ourselves, but, rather, to be part of something that has
power, history, continuity, and a sustaining beauty larger than what
we can by ourselves create."*

*Ah! A paradox. We need to commit to institutions and care for
them, which seems at first glance like restriction. But at the same
time, these communities provide us with a grounding that allows us
to become our true selves. Perhaps it is like a favorite Unitarian
Universalist hymn suggests, "Roots hold me close. Wings set me free."
Aikman touches on an important point for any individual or congregation. When we feel anxious about resources, we tend to clutch
onto what we have, even to hoard it. Doing so never liberates us,
however. Only generosity sets us free. We look to our religious communities to remind us of that central spiritual truth. In turn, we*

must remember that our congregations, too, need to escape the bonds of anxiety over resources. It is up to us, and the generosity we can bring out in others, to teach them to fly. —S. M.

∼

THREE YEARS AGO, when I was new around these parts, my friend Brian invited me to play racquetball with him at the YMCA. I had not played in ages and so asked him if he had an extra racquet. He said no but suggested I should get myself one. "They're only about twenty dollars," he said.

Well, at that point, I was just getting on my feet financially and in every other way; plus I wasn't sure whether I would play much. Twenty dollars sounded like a significant sum. So I went to the thrift store and poked around, and I bought a racquet for the grand sum of ninety-nine cents. Once I wrapped masking tape around the sticky handle, it was perfectly serviceable.

It was not a very good racquet, but it was good enough for me, and I was reasonably happy with it for quite some time. I seldom played anyway. Then I joined the Y, and this past summer, my friend Michele and I started playing pretty regularly. Later, playing with some other people, I matured as a player, growing able to play strategically and to pace myself, to capitalize on my opponents' weaknesses. As my skills improved, I began to see the shortcomings of my racquet and to yearn for a new one.

Then Christmas came, and both of my regular opponents got new racquets. The advantage of having a technically improved racquet started to reflect itself in the scores. I am not a fanatic, but I do write down the scores on this little computer-generated grid I keep on the bulletin board in my kitchen. Soon, I noticed that I was starting to lose more games than I was winning. There was no doubt about it; I needed a better racquet if my scores were going to improve. But since the old one really worked just fine, I found it hard to justify spending twenty or thirty dollars on a racquet for myself.

As I delve into the subject of money, I uncover a great deal of anxiety inside myself. I come across a feeling that there isn't enough and there never will be enough. When I feel this way, a great desire for control takes hold of me. I call this my Scottish genes acting up, but really, I think it has been learned. At times, I react to this anxiety by trying to clutch onto every cent I can, becoming jealous and protective of my money. Generosity eludes me.

Similarly, there are times when I feel overwhelmed by all the demands on me—emotional, administrative, all the things I am longing to do—and unlike many of you, I do not even have family responsibilities, or a pet, or even—now that I have killed off most of my housewarming gifts—very many plants. (Two particularly tenacious plants have now survived three months of my ministrations, and I'm beginning to suspect they are made of some artificial material.) When I get caught up in that feeling of being overwhelmed and exhausted, it's difficult for me to be generous with my time or my emotional presence. I start clutching onto every moment I can; I become jealous and protective of my time.

Overwhelmed. Exhausted. Maybe even ready to give up. That pretty much describes the way Everett Unitarian Universalist Fellowship was in the early 1980s. After three decades of being a flourishing lay-led fellowship, the congregation had dwindled down to twenty-one people. In the 1960s, the religious education program had had an enrollment of over sixty kids, but now there were no children at all. By 1983, it had become clear that the Fellowship was threatened with terminal illness. The members had to face the fact that one of their options was to close their doors permanently.

In 1983, however, a few core members of the Everett Fellowship attended a district extension program on growth. When they returned, they resolved not to let the Fellowship die. They also decided not simply to hoard, not to clutch onto the little they had left. Instead, they would let go, take a risk, make the leap of faith.

They spent a weekend envisioning and making plans for the future of the Fellowship. As they did, they grew excited about the possibilities. And—this is the key—people started making financial commitments to the Fellowship.

Then they did something that might have seemed illogical. With no kids in the religious education program, they hired two teachers. For several Sundays, the teachers did nothing; there were no children to teach. But then, as news spread that religious education was starting up again at the Fellowship, children started to arrive, and they brought their parents. The Fellowship began to grow again. From a membership of thirty-five and a budget of $10,000 in 1985, the Fellowship has grown to a membership of 116 and a budget of over $100,000. It happened because of the leap of faith on the part of those core members, the refusal to clutch on to the little they had, the willingness to step into the unknown.

I, too, found a willingness to take the plunge. I finally went out shopping a few weeks ago, on payday, for a new racquet. I stood in front of a huge display at SportMart, which had racquets ranging from $20 to $150 and some even more expensive than that. I picked one out. It looked pretty good, and it felt pretty good. It certainly wasn't the top of the line, but it wasn't the bottom either. I felt a fondness for it right away.

Recently, I had the funniest sensation. As I went to put my briefcase in the trunk of my car, I saw my new racquet, and I felt this great desire to grasp the handle. It wasn't just for the physical pleasure of holding it. As I examined the feeling, the strangest words came to me: This is how you fly. Flying! With a racquetball racquet? But that is it. This racquet helps me fly.

One of the most important spiritual lessons I am learning, over and over again, is that when I stop hoarding and clutching and protecting myself, I can fly. When I started playing racquetball, I protected myself from any extreme effort. I missed half my shots simply because I did not believe I could get to them. In fact,

I believed I would hurt myself if I went after them, that I would deplete myself if I tried too hard.

Now that I have matured in my playing, I am much more daring. Every now and then, when I am playing as hard as I can against a well-matched opponent, *I can do things that I couldn't believe I could do.* I reach a ball that is hit into some remote corner of the room, and I literally do not know how I got there. I come to the edge of what I thought I knew about my physical capabilities and find that my feet do not seem even to touch the floor. I am aware of nothing but the intensity of the moment. It really does feel like flying.

In my work, when I can let go of my worries about how I am coming across or how good a job I am doing, or how much emotional energy or time something is taking, it also feels like flying. You know that feeling—when you are one with the thing you are doing, time melts away, and there is an extraordinary feeling of freedom. You get in touch with a wild generosity of spirit inside yourself. It is exhilarating.

I think those flying moments come when there is true ministry, deep listening, going on between people—during the hush at Joys and Concerns, the hubbub in a children's religious education class, deep sharing in the men's group, a group conversation at a circle supper, a moment of hilarity during a Board meeting. When we forget ourselves and enter totally into the moment, the fellowship, the conversation—that is where the holy dwells.

People go to church for many reasons. For many of us, it is because we have come to the edge of all the light we have. We long for something solid to stand upon. And many churches, many healthy religious communities, offer that solid ground. There is a seemingly solid center to their belief systems that gives people something to stand upon.

Last week, I was at our district meeting in Vancouver and had the privilege of being in on some conversations with John Buehrens, the president of the Unitarian Universalist Association. We were speculating about the future of our movement, and the question arose, "What is the center of our faith?" John said ours is not a faith with a center; ours is a faith of *radical hospitality*, a radically inclusive witness in an exclusionary world, the core identity of which lies in the quality of the relationships we have with one another.

I would add that Unitarian Universalism does not offer something solid we can stand upon—no dogma, no creed, no blessed assurances, no ironclad foursquare rocks of ages. It offers something else. *It teaches us to fly by giving us what we need to respond to the urgings of the Spirit*—permission, a sustaining philosophy, a faith in the goodness of the quest. And this fellowship supports that by giving us a launch pad, a safe and nurturing base from which to take off and to which we can return.

I paid an entry fee when I joined the YMCA, and I now pay dues of $35 a month. It seems well worth it for what I get. There are no entry fees or dues at the Fellowship, however. When the questions of pledging minimum amounts or of charging tuition for our religious education program have come before the Board or the congregation, they have been defeated. There is no "fee for services" plan here, as there is at some mega-churches. I pledge as a percentage of my salary and housing allowance. This current year, I'm pledging 2.5 percent, or about $66, a month. For this coming year, I have raised that to 3 percent, or about $1,129, for the year.

It is a stretch for me, quite frankly. But in balance, it seems well worth it for what I get—a sense of ownership, a conviction that I am pulling my weight, the knowledge that I am contributing to the larger movement, to the faith that nurtures me, and to the institution that sustains my faith.

When I went to the district meeting and picked up my registration materials, along with my name badge, I got these ribbons. This one means that I was a ministerial delegate, entitled to vote at the business meeting on behalf of this fellowship. This one means that this fellowship is a full-share honor society in the District. And finally, this one means that this fellowship is a member of the UUA's Annual Program Fund Honor Society.

The Fellowship pays its full dues to the District and the UUA, based on the number of our members, and so these ribbons really belong to all of you. This means that no matter what the other demands on your budget have been, this congregation has, time and time again, chosen to pay its Fair Share to the larger movement in which we have our being.

During the annual banquet on Saturday night, I was engaged in a riveting conversation with my colleague Elizabeth Greene, and in the middle of it, she started snickering at me. "What's up?" I asked. "You're wiping your mouth on your ribbons," she said. So there might be a little gravy on there. But it was just a momentary lapse, and it did not mean I was not very proud to wear these ribbons, because I certainly was.

I am inspired by Unitarian Universalism. I am inspired by you, by your generosity. Of the twenty-seven Unitarian Universalist churches in the state of Washington, the per-capita giving of this congregation is among the top seven. This congregation is mature. It is a mark of maturity to support the institutions you believe in.

Institution is not a very thrilling word. But what it means to me is freedom. The freedom not to have to keep re-inventing ourselves but, rather, to be part of something that has power, history, continuity, and a sustaining beauty larger than what we can by ourselves create.

There is a *Non Sequitur* cartoon that shows a man sitting at a table on a city sidewalk with what looks like a petition on the table and an arrow saying, "Sign up here." Next to the table is a large wooden sign with a thermometer graphic on it. The poster is headed, "Join and help us reach our goal!" At the top level of the thermometer is the goal, "Mainstream Religion," followed by "Sect," "Faction," "Cult," "Bunch of Nuts" near the bottom, and at the very bottom, "Handful of Wackos."

I am very glad that core group of members decided in 1983 not to be content with letting the Everett Unitarian Universalist Fellowship remain a Handful of Wackos but had the faith that it could grow, and mature, and adopt a new regional identity, renaming itself the Evergreen UU Fellowship. I am glad they decided to become what our mission statement describes, a "liberal religious home where people find a welcoming community, a stimulating place of learning and worship, and the challenge and support to live the Unitarian Universalist Principles and Purposes."

Before I became serious about racquetball, when my old racquet seemed good enough, I found playing to be a lot of hard work, kind of boring even. It took a considerable amount of devotion, practice, and maturation to get to the stage where I was able to feel I deserved a good racquet, to the stage where I was, at last, able to fly. I found that when you play as hard as you can, who wins the point does not really matter very much. What matters is the flying, the passion, the wild generosity of spirit. Giving our all, in the moment, is what creates the delight. As an anonymous poet says,

> When we come to the edge of all the light we have
> And we step into the darkness, the unknown
> We will find something solid we can stand upon
> Or I believe that we will surely learn to fly.
>   So may it be for all of us. Amen.

~

Personal Reflection

What stood between Amanda Aikman and a new racquet was not only financial hardship but also a feeling that she did not deserve one. When have you been stopped, internally, from reaching more generously toward your own possibilities? What, if anything, liberated you?

For the Congregation

1. Amanda Aikman draws a parallel between the way that a new racquet allowed her to reach greater heights in her racquetball game and the way a particular congregation realized new possibilities by taking a risk. What leaps could your congregation make that might help it find new life?

2. Fear nearly prevented Aikman from playing her best game. She did not absolutely require a new racquet, and she assumed she did not deserve one. Is your congregation being prevented from moving ahead with its dreams by any unstated assumptions?

MAKING A DIFFERENCE:
A THEOLOGY OF MONEY

REV. VIRGINIA P. KNOWLES

First Unitarian Church
Lynchburg, Virginia

Virginia Knowles' disarming confession that she was once one of the Unitarian Universalists who do not generously support their congregations carries us right to the heart of the fundraising challenge in our churches. Many of us do not think we are the ones who bear the responsibility to give more, yet who else is there?

Knowles further invites us to confront our frequent double standard in honoring the contributions people make. All of us readily acknowledge other kinds of gifts in our religious communities, but we balk, apologize, and rationalize when it comes to paying tribute to those who give of their financial resources. Her rational explication amounts to an invitation to do it differently.

The beauty of Knowles' sermon is that she uses her personal journey to represent the obstacles nearly every congregation and every church member or friend must overcome in order to give generously. Many readers will find a familiar story in this clear and insightful sermon. —S. M.

IN THE BELIEF that phylogeny follows a path similar to that of ontogeny, and in the hope that my personal evolution may be typical of the evolution of some of you in this congregation, I begin with a personal story.

As a religious education director thirty-five years ago, I wanted no part in the pledge drives. This involved asking people for money. My part in the life of the church was to see that the children and adults received good religious education, personally and in a class. My work was with counseling and curriculum, aesthetics and personal growth. The mundane job of asking people for money was for someone else. Curiously, I was never challenged in this view.

I left religious education and started afresh in a new government agency. I was then the primary support of my family and didn't have much money. The good members of my church who canvassed me understood this and accepted my meager financial contribution as one might have accepted the widow's mite. I made substantial contributions in time and energy, and we were all comfortable.

My salary rose. It never occurred to me to increase my pledge to the church that was so important in my life and in the lives of my children. My children grew up and moved away. I had no particular money worries. I had a once-a-week maid and took trips abroad. It never occurred to me to increase my pledge to the church I loved and of which I was an active member. And no one ever suggested to me directly that I might consider doing so.

When I began to study to be a minister and understood more about church dynamics and church finances, my attitude changed radically. I remember that the first week of my internship in Rockford, Illinois, I was asked to attend a meeting of the Planning Committee for the pledge drive and the budget because I needed to learn the part a minister can play to make the drive a success. I actually enjoyed this, and I have ever since. It didn't take me long to appreciate that there can be no separation between what a church can offer its members and its community and that church's budget.

The budget determines, to a large extent, the strength of a congregation. The strength of a congregation determines how much it can give its members and how much it can reach out into the larger community. How much difference we make in the world is the function of our energy and time and creativity and money—all of these.

Ministers and religious educators must be vitally concerned with how much is raised in a pledge drive because their work for the spiritual health of their congregation is directly affected. Money is involved in offering inspiring sermons and speakers. Money is involved in the quality of seminars and support groups. Money is involved in the number and quality of visits and other contacts a church community can have with those who are bereaved or homebound or ill. Money is involved in the kind of music that is offered. Money is involved in the education of our children. Money is involved in the effectiveness of our communications, our internal and external public relations. Money is involved in the beauty and accessibility and visibility of our buildings. Money is involved in our work in helping those in our community who are less fortunate than we are.

At first glance this might seem in contrast with what I said in September about the edifice complex. But it isn't. Energy and time and creativity and love—all these are essential. Commitment, creativity, energy, caring, and money together determine the spiritual life of a church.

I decided that a sermon on the theology of money was an appropriate follow-up to the sermon on the edifice complex. We Unitarian Universalists tend to have a money complex. We feel free to talk and talk about the need for volunteers to make coffee, teach in the religious education program, conduct a Sunday service, care for the grounds, be a committee chair, contribute food for the Gateway Inn. We applaud our members who can sing or play a musical instrument. Yet we cringe at applauding those who support our religious beliefs by giving large sums of money. We opine that those who cannot give much will feel hurt. This doesn't make sense, much less dollars. Most of us can't sing or play a musical instrument well enough to participate in a church service, but this doesn't prevent us from celebrating those who can. It doesn't prevent us from printing their names in the order of service. Virtually all of our churches devote a portion of a service every year to honoring outstanding volunteers, and sometimes those who are not particularly outstanding. Do we give public recognition to those who are outstanding in the amount of money they give? A few churches do this, and their number is increasing. Those who truly cannot give much in money applaud, figuratively, those who can and do. Making money the exception when we express the church's appreciation for every other contribution to its life seems to me like a kind of inverse snobbishness.

Studies show that Unitarian Universalists have the greatest per capita income of any denomination, but we have the lowest per capita rate of giving. Yet we lament the political influence of the churches that raise more money in order to have that influence. I suggest that one reason we have a low rate of giving is that we find it so hard to talk about money and to celebrate it as a morally applaudable channel through which to live out our religious convictions. Virtually *none* of our leaders hesitates to try to persuade members to give more time to the church by taking on this or that job. "I twisted her arm" is frequently and proudly spoken in our churches. Yet almost never do we talk candidly with another member about the virtue of giving as much as possible in dollars.

Money is recognized as "the bottom line" in our culture. Our alma maters, our symphonies—all our cultural and non-profit agencies—print lists of patrons and sponsors and friends, lists that specify the giving range in which people have chosen to be. Yet the same people who urge us to give to the United Givers Fund until it hurts—or until it feels good, according to the slogan in vogue that year—these same people usually freeze at the notion of personally and directly urging someone to give more to the church, particularly if it's a Unitarian Universalist church.

I understand this feeling. Do you know that this is the first sermon I have ever given directly urging people to give more money? I did write a church newsletter column once urging the church to give its full share to the denomination. This plea was successful. When the congregation was reminded of the many gifts we receive from the Unitarian Universalist Association, its members realized that the church could not exist without the denomination. No one in that congregation really wanted to be a freeloader. I'm still embarrassed when I remember not raising my pledge to my church twenty-five years ago.

I have come to appreciate that encouraging you to give money is as proper a function for a minister as encouraging you to be courageous or honest or more concerned with social action. Hear what a few of the world's great thinkers have said about giving.

Kahlil Gibran: "You have often heard it said, 'I would give, but only to the deserving.' The trees in your orchard say not so, nor the flocks of your pasture. They give that they may live, for to withhold is to perish."

Mohammed: "Our true wealth is the good we do in the world. None of us has faith unless we desire for our neighbors what we desire for ourselves."

William James: "The great use of a life is to spend it for something that outlasts it."

I have been troubled for years that we are such poor givers. I find no evidence that we care less about our church and our religion than other churches. For fifty years, I have participated in seminars and private discussions in which people have testified to their joy when they discovered Unitarian Universalism: "a religion where I can say what I think," "a place where I can be myself," "a church that doesn't try to scare me into being good," "a religion that urges me to use my reason." In our quieter way, we demonstrate the same commitment and fervor that those in revival meetings do—but not the same fervor in pledging.

I have several orthodox Christian friends who tithe. These particular people do not do so because they fear retribution if they do not. They give 10 percent of their income to their religious communities because they believe it is the right thing to do. When I reported on my trip to Korea with the International Association of Religious Freedom, I told about the Japanese woman in my circle group who told us, with tears in her voice, that she had met someone who had received food purchased by her religious group's weekly Donate a Meal project. She was so moved by the difference they had made that she wanted Risho Kosei Kai members to go without meals two times a week. I told about the Won Buddhist nun with whom I spent an evening. She had somehow collected millions of dollars from around the world to do everything from building schools in remote areas to distributing food on a regular basis. One of you asked me, "What makes people give so much to her for her projects?" My sense is that she is so enthusiastic and committed to her work, and so willing to tell everyone about the difference this makes in the lives of children and women and men, that people want to be a part of it.

Sometimes languishing young people's groups are revitalized when they are mobilized to do something that makes a difference in the world outside themselves. I believe that most of us, young and old, would like to make a difference in the world. If we contribute generously to a cause that will have a lasting effect for good in the world after we ourselves are gone from it, we achieve the only immortality in which most of us Unitarian Universalists believe.

We know that as a religious community, we can make a greater difference in the world than each of us could make working alone. I like the simile of the Canadian geese. Some of you know why they always fly in a V. Aerodynamic engineers wondered about this for years until they discovered the reason from experiments in a wind tunnel. Each goose, in flapping its wings, creates an upward lift for the goose that follows. So when all the geese do their part in the V formation, the whole flock has a 70 percent greater flying range than if each bird flew alone. Furthermore, when a goose begins to lag behind, the others "honk" it back into place. And when the goose at the head or the V gets tired, another goose shifts position and takes over from it.

So, if you really can't increase your pledge this year because you need the money for food and shelter, or whatever, don't feel bad. Someone else will be able to make an extra increase in his or her pledge. Like the geese, each of us has a function in the flock, but it is a different function at different times. We each give in the area where we are strong at any particular time.

I reviewed the Principles and Purposes of the Unitarian Universalist Association, to which we all belong. When we sign the membership book of a church, we indirectly agree to support these Principles because every UU church is a member of the UUA. I was looking for a clue as to why our support of our religion is not at a higher level. I found no clue—rather, the opposite. The Principles and Purposes of our Unitarian Universalist Association, which we as a member congregation covenant to affirm, are expensive.

I know that we're too smart to interpret references to a free church and a free pulpit to mean no one has to pay. And in the fourth Principle, "A free and responsible search for truth and meaning," the word "responsible" clearly indicates that the "free" does not imply abnegation of obligation.

The second Principle, "Justice, equity, and compassion in human relations"; the fifth Principle, which includes, "The right of conscience and the use of the democratic process in the world at large"; and the sixth Principle, "The goal of world community with peace, liberty, and justice for all"—these strike me as demanding a great deal of time, energy, creativity, and money, if we are to follow through on our commitment to them.

I have heard unflattering verbal cartoons about Unitarian Universalists: "The one miracle Unitarian Universalists believe in is that the Lord will provide." "The only dirty word in the UU church is *money*." A little of this kind of humor goes a long way. It is not fair to those dedicated members and friends who plan and scheme how to give to their religion as much money and time and energy and love as they possibly can. Nor does it properly honor our religious ancestors who sacrificed their homes and careers, even their families, and sometimes their lives, for the only faith to which they could give their wholehearted commitment. Without their sacrifice, we would not be here this morning, sitting more or less comfortably among our peers, free to disagree openly with one another, to disagree openly with the Unitarian Universalist Association, and to disagree openly with the minister.

We know that we support what we value. I had considered reading to you what other Unitarian Universalists have said about why we come to church. But you know better than anyone else why you are here. I invite you to take a few quiet moments at this time to concentrate, prayerfully if you will, on what would be missing from your life if this church and Unitarian Universalism were not in the world.

So be it.

$\sim$

Personal Reflection

How are you supporting what you value in your life right now? Have you ever felt that you weren't doing your fair share? What difference has the recognition made in your life?

For the Congregation

1. Consider all the ways your congregation honors the members

who support its work and its life. Do you give as much acknowledgment to those who show their support monetarily? If not, what might you do to change that? How might you explain the changes so that the entire congregation will embrace this recognition?

2. Why are we comfortable recognizing that some people have a musical gift, or artistic gift, or educational talent, but uncomfortable suggesting that some are more gifted in their financial resources? Does wealth indicate something about worth or success that is not true of other gifts? Does this speak to money's "dirtiness," or its power, or both?

CAUTION CHURCH AHEAD

Rev. Victoria Safford

The Unitarian Society of Northampton and Florence
Northampton, Massachusetts

Victoria Safford faces head-on the frequent accusation that liberal religion really does not ask much of its participants. We don't demand dues or tithes; we don't ask for confession of sins; we don't require confession of creeds—the list goes on. One would think that we perpetuate cautious churches.

In reality, though, what we ask is much deeper and more demanding. In Safford's elegant, simple language, we ask our people to become one another's shelter, and she brings it down to the realities of religious education, pastoral care, and fundraising. Living in a time when black-and-white theological doctrines are held as truth and religion is defined narrowly, we do well to remember the depth and importance of the religious claims upon us. Safford reminds us of that and more. She demonstrates that liberal religion makes profound demands of us. The rest is up to us. –S. M.

What then is sanctuary? The sanctuary is often something very small. Not a grandiose gesture, but a small gesture toward alleviating human suffering and preventing humiliation. The sanctuary is a human being. Sanctuary is a dream. And that is why you are here and that is why I am here. We are here because of one another. We are in truth each other's shelter.

—Elie Wiesel

This is not metaphorical language. This *is* exactly true. We are each other's shelter. We are each other's sanctuary. This is ethical language, this is spiritual language, and in so far as it calls us to community, it is religious language. From the raging, crazy storms of secular society, from the hatred and confusion that abounds out there, from the loneliness and sorrow and terrors that are inevitable, we are each other's shelter; we are each other's sanctuary. This house is for the ingathering of those who believe it, those who thrive under that generous premise, and those who are aching for the embrace of that sheltering promise.

From time to time, someone around here will casually admit that what they really like about this congregation—this society, this church—about Unitarian Universalism, is that it asks so little of him. And the response is, "But friend, we ask you to be each other's shelter. We ask you to be sanctuary to each other. We ask you to be human beings."

We ask you to care for each other, to notice when illness strikes, or death, or sorrows invisible. We ask you to be a community. We know it's hard when you first come, and there are four hundred people in the room, and you don't know a single one of them, but this is what we ask.

We ask you to help one another to teach each other's children (morally, ethically, spiritually) and to teach each other to be wise parents. We ask you to prepare meals for each other, to drive each other here when one of you is seventy and one of you is not. We ask you to look out for each other.

We ask you to risk confessing your faith to each other, which first means to risk finding it. We ask you to conduct the search of a lifetime, with integrity and courage, to wrestle God to the ground and tell us in the morning who won. We ask you to abandon easy, blind beliefs and dare to discover your own questions.

We ask you to defend free faith, to understand that this is a rare and rather fragile place, a temple of free speech, dedicated to spiritual pluralism, to intellectual wandering, and to mystical wondering. We ask you to defend free faith, which these days is no easy task. When we are called heretics, blasphemers, pagans, we ask you to clear your throat and stand up and say, "Guilty as charged and proud of it!" We ask *you* to stand up and say, "And we, too, have a worthy faith. And we, too, have family values. And we, too, have good news to preach to the masses."

We ask you to run this place. We ask that you not succumb to the temptation to leave things in the dubious and shaky hands of the clergy, but to claim ownership—to love the building till it shines, to organize the committees and join them and chair them and envision for them a worthy mission. We ask you to pour the coffee and come to the work parties, to fold the newsletter and deliver the flowers. (Who do you think is going to do these things?) We ask you to understand the budget and the bylaws and the congregational polity by which we are governed, and which clearly states that all authority here, and all responsibility, emanate from the laity, from the people, from the pew. We ask you to buy into that.

We ask you outright to celebrate our pride in being a Welcoming Congregation. Whatever your own sexual orientation, we ask you outright to celebrate the gay, lesbian, bisexual, heterosexual rainbow we've become. We ask you to celebrate our gay and lesbian families and all the other families. We ask you to understand that to celebrate is to bear witness, and to bear witness is sometimes to greet hatred and ignorance with some measure of appropriate rage and appropriate dignity. We ask you to stand tall.

We ask you to be prophets in your own land and to practice your religion actively beyond these walls, seven days a week. We ask you to erase the lines between the contemplative life and the active life, the so-called spiritual and the so-called political. We ask for embodied faith.

And what else? We ask that you usher once in a while—since someone has to do it—that you come to the annual meeting, that you help out at the tag sale in the spring and the picnic in the fall, and basically that you look at your life in this community as exactly that, life within community. We ask you to know that unless each of you who takes a seat on Sunday is engaged here, hand and heart and head, there's a danger the place may collapse under the weight of us all. We ask you to be at home here, with all that that implies.

There's a sign posted somewhere out on Routes 2 and 202, way out there near Gardner, Winchendon, Petersham, on the far side of the Quabbin Reservoir, near a fairly sharp curve. The sign says, Caution Church Ahead. In today's Order of Meeting, I see a colon has crept in, but this is a typo. On the actual sign, there is no punctuation, just "Caution Church Ahead."

And so you wonder, driving by, craning your neck for a view, are they the "caution church"—the cautious church, afraid to say anything, afraid to do anything, afraid to take a stand, afraid of God, afraid of strangers, cautious and careful, pious and practical? It's not a very inviting sign. Or is the sign posted as a warning, in fact warranting a colon: "Caution: Church Ahead"? There's a lot to be scared of in churches these days. One would do well, no doubt, to round that curve carefully. I'm not sure that we need so flamboyant and ambiguous a sign, but perhaps something could be posted outside that says, if not "Caution Church Ahead," then maybe "Watch Out! Unitarian Universalists Ahead! They Ask That You Take It Seriously. They Ask a Lot of You in There."

Without it, the person I'm talking to, the one who said that what he likes about the place is that we don't ask for much, will stare at me for a moment or two, chewing on this little speech I've just made, and then say, "Yeah, but you don't really ask for anything. You don't ask for dues. You don't ask for a tithe. You don't ask for money a lot. You don't make us feel guilty." And the response is, "But, friend, we ask you to be each other's shelter, to be each other's sanctuary. Listen hard. Read the sign. We're asking a great deal of you."

We ask that you weave here, together, some kind of sturdy, gorgeous web, because without that among you, the building doesn't stand. There's no sanctuary here that is not made of your flesh and bone and love and will. The building will not stand. The ministry won't stand. The staff fall down. The lights go out. Religious education shuts down, and the kids are on their own in the wild world. The thing won't work. So, yes, we ask you to fund it.

Whether you're a member of the Society, or whether you just come on Sunday mornings; whether you come alone or with several children for our Sunday School; whether you rush in and out or stay for potlucks and programs and counseling and the rest, we ask you every year for a financial pledge. And because "we" are "you," we can be neither apologetic nor coy nor subtle about this.

It's said that when Andrew Carnegie, the industrialist turned philanthropist, began giving away his fortune, many people were moved, understandably, to write him letters. He got one such letter from his friend, Mark Twain. It said,

> You seem to be in prosperity. Could you lend an admirer a dollar and a half to buy a hymn-book with? God will bless you. I feel it. I know it. P. S. Don't send the hymn-book, send the money.

We ask you, without apology, to send the money. We (meaning you) ask you to pay for the Unitarian Society of Northampton and Florence because, quite frankly, no one else and nothing else will. Guilt has nothing to do with it. We ask that you be each other's shelter, that you be each other's sanctuary.

In an interview some years ago, writer Annie Dillard spoke about how she constructed her memoir, *An American Childhood*. She's comparing the work of writing a book to raising a child, but she could as easily be talking about life in a community like this one:

> Willpower has very little to do with it. If you have a little baby crying in the middle of the night, and if you depend only on willpower to get you out of bed to feed the baby, that baby will starve. You do it out of love. Willpower is a weak idea; love is strong. You don't have to scourge yourself with a cat-o-nine-tails to go to the baby. You go to the baby out of love for that particular baby. That's the same way you go to your desk [or I might say, the way you come to church]. There's nothing freakish about it. Caring passionately about something isn't against nature, and it isn't against human nature. It's what we're here to do.

Willpower is a weak idea, says Annie Dillard. And guilt is a weak idea; babies are not fed in the night because of weak ideas like guilt. Liberal congregations are not funded and supported on weak ideas like guilt. They thrive on love and passionate caring, and the money comes accordingly. Caring about something is what we're here to do.

For most, though not all of us, in this room, money is nothing but a string of choices made one after another after another. For some few of us in this room who survive on AFDC and food stamps, and a quick wit, and a wing and a prayer, there are no choices, but for most of us, let's face it, money represents decision-making power. Even if we live from paycheck to paycheck, even if much of that paycheck is servicing debts, even if there is never enough money, still we are making choices.

We decide what kind of housing we "need" to have, and then we decide to pay for it. It may mean a burdensome mortgage or a burdensome rent, but we do decide. We decide what kind of car, and how many cars, we need to drive, and then we decide to pay for them. We decide about private school for children, and dancing lessons and music lessons and art and soccer and so on, and then we decide to pay. We decide what our style is and pay for the clothes. We decide how many accoutrements we "need," which home computer, which VCR, which movies, which phone system, which furniture, which subscriptions, which foods, and we decide to pay for them.

More often than not, we frame these decisions in terms of what we "need," though the fact is, we need almost none of these things. We need a dry place to sleep, a certain number of calories per day, clothing to protect us from whatever New England dishes out, and that's it. And for some few of us in this room, and for some great uncounted number out there, that really is it. There are parents in this society who raise their kids with those needs, and no others, in mind. Not "I need a vacation." Not "I need some shoes to go with this dress." Not "I need that book, that CD, that software, that decaf from Bart's." Our desires and our decisions may be boundless, but our needs, if we're honest, are really pretty basic. We need shelter and food and clothing.

And beyond this, we need friendship.

We need comrades in the struggle.

We need art. We need a way to hear music often.

We need noble work, paid or unpaid, in the home or out of it; we need, each of us, a calling.

We need trees and grass and water fairly close by.

We need religious grounding. Some of us need a mature and sustaining experience of God. Some need prayer. Some need glimpses of the transcendent, a sense of something larger than themselves. Some of us need ethical clarity.

We need religious grounding.

We need solitude.

We need community.

We find the sources of these things we need, and then we choose to sustain them, to nurture them, not by willpower, not by some sense of duty or obligation, but because we care passionately about them and find them central to our lives.

We ask a lot of you here, but the things we ask are simple and straightforward. We ask that you fund this free-standing congregation to the extent that you're able and the extent that it touches you. But more importantly, we ask that you find and create sanctuary here. "Sanctuary," says Wiesel,

> is often something very small. Not . . . grandiose, but a small gesture toward alleviating human suffering and preventing humiliation. The sanctuary is a human being. Sanctuary is a dream. And that is why you are here and that is why I am here. We are here because of one another. We are in truth each other's shelter.

Much is asked of us in this liberal religious community. For me, as a member of the congregation and as a contributor to its budget, the joy lies in a wonderful paradox: The gifts demanded of me here are the very gifts I've been seeking my whole life long. We are asked to offer our laughter, our compassion, our reason, our faith, our best hope, and our humanity. And once a year, we're asked to offer money too.

I close with the words of John Winthrop, Puritan founder of the Massachusetts Bay Colony, and in a roundabout way, one of our spiritual ancestors. He wrote these words in 1630:

> We must be knit together in this work as one. . . . We must be willing to abridge ourselves of our superfluities, for the supply of others' necessities. . . . We must delight in each other, make each other's conditions our own, rejoice together, mourn together, labor and suffer together, always having before our eyes our community as members of the same body.

Amen.

~

Personal Reflection

When has someone else been your shelter? When have you provided shelter to another person? If you take it seriously, what does your liberal religion ask of you?

For the Congregation

1. As you welcome newcomers to your congregation, you surely lay out the privileges of membership and the joys of being part of a Unitarian Universalist community. You may even have long-term members speak of what they have gained from the church over the years. When do you suggest to these new pilgrims what the church and the religion will ask of them? Do you do it with apology? If so, what message does that convey?

2. As parents, workers, political activists, partners, and spouses, we rather relish how much commitment and thought and maturity the journey requires. Yet when it comes to our liberal religious communities, we seem to want the task to be inexpensive, not only in terms of money but in time, brainpower, and energy. Why do you think there is a disconnect between religion and the rest of our lives? Is there a way to bridge the gap in your congregation?

3. What would happen in your congregation if the discussion changed from, "what we can and cannot afford" to "what we choose to fund"? What does your congregation choose to fund, and what does it choose not to fund? What might it choose to fund in the future?

THE ENERGY OF ACTION: THE DUTY OF UNITARIAN UNIVERSALISM

DAVID A. DOMINA

Second Unitarian Universalist Church
Omaha, Nebraska

David Domina applies the term of his title to the fundamental driving force in our liberal religion. Sharing our vision and our values is, as he sees it, an imperative with a nearly evangelical mandate. He states, "The 'energy of action' means we, as Unitarian Universalists, have a deep, deep, duty. Our obligation is to keep the fire burning and to light it where it doesn't burn. Always." When we are tired and when we are angry. When we are offended and when we are content. Ours is a duty to question, to challenge, to demand. It is a duty to make a real difference in the lives of those around us, a duty to have an impact and to enrich the evolving history of all people, not to detract from it.

For any who might not be familiar with Unitarian Universalist history, this sermon offers the basics. Here, Domina introduces Michael Servetus, Francis David, Thomas Starr King, and Olympia Brown, all heroes or heroines of liberal religion who gave their energy —and in Servetus' case, his life—for the cause of keeping alive the flame of freedom. The preacher calls on us to be inspired by their examples and do our own part for our fiery faith. We can be grate-ful that Domina shares freely with us his enthusiasm for this tradi-tion. Sermons like this help to keep the chalice lit. –S. M.

∿

FIRE!
FIRE!
Enough for a mob scene!
A firebomb.
Enough for terror.
Let's have a fire . . . enough for a love scene.
A campfire . . . enough for a fellowship.

WHAT A MYSTERIOUS, frightening, yet alluring and reassuring thing. Fire. Is it a wonder that we have chosen it as the central focus of our worship? The object of the most consistent, reverent ritual in our religion. It is fire we create, each Sunday, when "we light this chalice . . . for the energy of action!"

Fire has almost universal religious significance. Since the beginning of human history, fire has been revered, used in wor-ship, and closely connected with the spiritual dimension of life. We Unitarians love to think our religion is so different. Some might call us a little smug, perhaps. But there it is at the core of our worship too—fire!

What does it mean? Fire is associated in our church with warmth of love, light of truth, and with today's focus, the energy of action. It reminds us of Michael Servetus' death by burning at the stake for his "heresy" at Geneva in 1553. And it called our leader to our First World Summit of Unitarian Leaders at Budapest just three years ago. In each of these instances, fire served as a stark reminder of our duty as members of a religion with a dynamic history of courage, intelligence, principle, and conviction. Indeed, *fire is our symbol for action!*

What is the Unitarian Universalist "energy of action"?

As Unitarians, we have committed ourselves to some basic Principles. I know many prefer another word, but I'll call these Principles our Unitarian Creed. We believe in, affirm, and promise to promote:

— The inherent worth and dignity of every person;
— Justice, equity, and compassion in human relations;
— Acceptance of one another and encouragement to spiritual growth in our congregations;
— A free and responsible search for truth and meaning.

But there is more. As Universalists, we are committed to:

— The right of conscience and the use of the democratic process within our congregations and in society at large;
— The goal of world community with peace, liberty, and justice for all;
— Respect for our interdependent web of all existence of which we are a part.

These basic Principles, then, are the core of our Unitarian Universalist energy and our action.

What has this energy of action meant?

Our Unitarian history is a remarkable history of action. In the peaceful city of Geneva, our fiery leader Michael Servetus was so committed to furthering social justice and challenging the Roman Church's dogmatic presence that he was burned at the stake for alleged heresy. Now, Servetus didn't just show up, have coffee, and throw a dollar or two in the collection. He *died* for what he believed!

Francis David and John Biddle suffered banishment and death for daring to fan the flames of religious persecution when they declared their belief in one God rather than a trinity. They gave more than time, more than talent, and more than worldly treasure.

They gave their lives for their commitment to the perception that it was Paul, the apostle, who invented the Trinity. Joseph Priestley withstood the heat of riots in England and condemnation in the New World to establish Unitarianism in North America.

It was *our* faith that fanned the flames of the American Revolution! Ours is the heritage of a faith held by Emerson, Thoreau, Whitman, Channing, and even Thomas Jefferson, who often called himself a Unitarian. They gave of themselves for what they believed.

We ordained the first woman in the recorded history of Judeo-Christian religion—Olympia Brown in 1863, sixty years before women could vote in this country.

The fire of commitment caused the Reverend Starr King to lead the Unitarians of San Francisco to advocate adoption of the Fourteenth and Fifteenth Amendments to the U. S. Constitution before their passage looked possible. And he invited black people to worship with white people, declaring nearly a century before the U. S. Supreme Court would do so in *Brown v. Topeka Board of Education* that separate is *not* equal—not to Unitarian Universalists. Starr King died young, but he accomplished more in his short life than all the contemporary ministers in his city in all their lives. He was committed, and he shared his commitment with the world.

Now that is fire! That's action.

What does this energy of action mean for us, now?

As Unitarian Universalists, we and our religion have survived without the promise of redemption or the guarantee of eternal life, without a creed, and without dogma in our worship. How? Why? Because our faith has been the faith of belief in people and possibilities. Ours is a faith that values thought, fosters debate, and demands action!

We believe in the energy of action. Indeed, we revere it! Ours is a fiery faith that trusts people and believes they are basically good. Ours is a doctrine of tolerance. We fervently believe that the only real liberal is a person who is open-minded, willing to listen, think, and be persuaded. And once persuaded, only a real liberal can kindle and fan the flames of genuine change into the all-consuming fire of life-altering reform.

So, what does *the energy of action* mean? Well, it means we have a heritage of doing and giving, not just saying or hearing. It means an active open-mindedness, a respect for humankind, and a fervent, fiery confidence that we can make a difference through what we do.

In short, *the energy of action* means we, as Unitarian Universalists, have a deep, deep, duty. Our obligation is to keep the fire burning and to light it where it doesn't burn, always—when we are tired and when we are angry; when we are offended and when we are content. Ours is a duty to question, to challenge, to demand. It is a duty to make a real difference in the lives of those around us. It is a duty to have an impact and to enrich the evolving history of all people, not to detract from it.

How does our duty relate to our lives as members of a congregation?

Today, we are gathered as a community of persons who share this fiery heritage and sense this duty to emblazon the emblem of our commitment to people and to democracy, to fairness and to dignity, on all we can touch. How, then, does this duty relate to our lives in this congregation? And what combustion can we ignite from this place, and as a community?

The focus now, for the rest of my time with you, is not on what we must do, for our causes can be many and varied. Rather, we must think now of the procedures of conflagration, the methods of ignition, and the tools we need as a congregation to move our smoldering community into a force of fire for social change.

How do we fuel the Unitarian heritage and feed the flame? What must we do to pass on the candescence of our faith? How can we ensure that the best and most historical moments of our religion lie before us and not in our heritage, behind us?

Well, first we must commit. Nothing short of commitment will work. Ours is not a religion of comfort, nor is it a practice of ivory-towered idealism. Michael Servetus must have felt so very real as he was threatened, beaten, and condemned. We must feel the flame of sacrificial reality just as he felt the real flames of fire claim his living flesh. We must give with the commitment that Servetus gave.

Second, we must share. We must pass on the dream of our faith and the heat of our passion for it. We cannot be a viable group of Unitarian Universalists committed to the Principles printed in our weekly *Worship Bulletin*—personal dignity, justice, acceptance, the right of conscience—unless we are willing to sacrifice with the fervor of Servetus too. Do you suppose Jefferson was comfortable writing the Declaration of Independence, knowing that bloodshed, including his own, was nearly inevitable? What about Thoreau, whose family was among the nation's wealthiest? Was he looking for the easy life by residing at Walden or by living out his essay on *Civil Disobedience*?

How can we hope to pass on the fire of this ancestry by letting our buildings suffer from lack of attention or letting our children go with a little less than is needed for their religious instruction? How can we pass on the Unitarian Universalist dream if we have a bit too little money for the quality of worship we need to strengthen our togetherness in the cause of social justice?

How can we feel the reality of Servetus and our heritage if we are content to fund the Unitarian Universalist dream only after we have paid the interest bill on our luxury credit card debt or whatever the competing item might be? How?

How, if we are content to let the courage of the past simply smolder on our shift, can we expect the Unitarian Universalists who follow us to ignite the dream into dynamic change?

So we must share, sacrificially. Money and time. Goals and ambitions. Ideas and actions. We must share, constantly, with each other and with others. If we stop, or if we share too little, the fire of our faith grows a bit dimmer. And, untended, after a time, the fire dies to cold embers, waiting to be sparked and fanned again by someone else, having been left to die by each of us.

This is our duty.

This is our duty, to commit and to share—here, as a congregation. You know, each of us can make a difference alone. But together, we can do even more. Numbers count. And together we can make more change, fan more flame, fuel more action, and ignite more thought than we possibly can by drifting off separately.

Oh, this does not mean we must *think* alike. But we must think! And it does not mean we must *act* alike. But we must act. We need not all show our *commitment* in the same way, but we must commit. And we must appreciate, together, our faith in the Principles for which our religion stands.

We must give time, talents, and treasures. We must give freely. We must be Unitarian Universalists to be agents of action, not to be *different*, or comfortable, and not just to belong. For us, this is a moral imperative. It is the thing for which we light our chalice each week. It is the energy of action.

∼

Personal Reflection

We do not have to think alike, says David Domina, "but we must think." We do not have to act alike, "but we must act." What would you like to spend your own fire on? If you could make one contribution toward keeping the flame of liberal religion burning during your lifetime, what would you like it to be?

For the Congregation

1.   David Domina calls Unitarian Universalists to claim and per-

petuate the legacy of action given to us by the great religious heroes of our past. What are the most important actions in which your congregation is currently involved? What is needed to fan the flame of that action so that it will burn even more intently?

2. Domina addresses priorities here. It is not enough to fund dreams only if there is something left after paying the usual bills. What kind of vision does it take to fund dreams? What kind of fund drive?

3. The two most important steps in tending the flame are committing and sharing. How do you address those two in your congregational life?

MONEY

REV. WEBSTER KITCHELL HOWELL
Unitarian Universalist Church
Lancaster, Pennsylvania

The argument Howell presents goes something like this. We have trouble truly realizing that there is nothing inherently dirty in money. All of the negative feelings and associations we develop around money derive not from its nature but from the way we use it. True freedom, then, consists of making intentional choices about how to use the resources with which we are blessed. Indeed, by making our money serve the higher, or deeper, values in which we believe, we even have the opportunity to make it sacred.

In 1997 I was called to serve the Unitarian Universalist Church of Lancaster, Pennsylvania. My ministry followed that of Kit Howell, who had died of cancer in 1996. Howell was greatly beloved in the Lancaster congregation, not least of all for his preaching. He had the gift of stimulating people's minds while also touching their hearts and transforming their lives. In this sermon, he exhibits the rare ability of a preacher to educate his listeners while challenging them to grapple with their most deeply held assumptions.

If you never want to think about money in the same way again, read this sermon. Who knows? Money might even end up speaking to you. —S. M.

THIS HAS NOT been an easy sermon for me. You have no idea how hard it is to come up with something to say about money at canvass time that doesn't sound like advertising. What can you say about money that lends itself to having people give to either this church or this denomination?

I pondered this issue until, finally, I went and got a dollar bill out of my wallet and interviewed it. What follows is our conversation.

"Well, hey, Money!" I say. "Thanks for coming by."

"No problem," says Money. "I can't stay long, though. You know I'm going to be out of your wallet and into somebody else's real soon."

"This won't take long," I say.

"Good," says Money. "You know, I sense a real ambivalence about you when it comes to me."

"That's right," I say. "I don't understand you at all."

"I know," says Money. "I can tell because you don't treat me very well. In fact, when you get scared, you squeeze me too tight; you try to hoard me. When you are in denial, you throw me around like you don't respect me, or even like you are trying to get rid of me."

"I know," I say. "I find you a bit scary altogether. I try to avoid thinking about you. Ask my wife. She asks me to look at the MasterCard bill and I flee in terror. You are very powerful, I know. For example, whenever my parents fought, it was about you. In fact, I think you were the image that carried my parents to divorce. You became an issue of power and control in their marriage."

"Actually," I say, becoming more self-confident, "it's hard to not feel your power in all of our market-oriented society. You flow through all human relationships, including our relationship with ourselves. You are everywhere, but we really don't acknowledge your pervasiveness. We will share the most intimate details of our lives with each other, but we don't talk about how much of *you* we have. We are ashamed when we don't have you, and we don't want to boast or tempt fate when we have plenty of you. You remain in the shadow of our consciousness, like a public taboo.

"You are so private and so public at the same time. You seem to catch us at our most vulnerable and our most base. When I have little money, it reminds me of my limitations, and when I have a lot of it, it lets me pretend I am omnipotent. When I have little money, it tells me I will have a hard time providing for my needs, a harder time providing for my wants, and an impossible time providing for my fantasies. So, if I don't have you, I feel trapped and ineffectual, as if life's possibilities are withheld from me, as if the 'ground of being' has been jerked right out from under me. So, yes, I am afraid of you! You are powerful stuff!

"You can take a normal person, capable of love, dignity, and compassion, and with your absence or presence, turn him into a cornered animal. You can make us feel so small and vulnerable that we might lash out in fear and hurt someone we love. This is called 'arguing over money.' Most of us have done that. Even churches do that. It's when the money gets tight around here that we start blaming and pointing fingers at each other. People can do some really bad things to each other when you are involved."

And here I start to really get into it. I go on, "I think we all pretty much accept that you can be tied, through our needs and fears, to what is lowest in us. You make us greedy, selfish, and retentive. As such, those of us who are *sensitive* are almost embarrassed by you. You are a kind of cultural body function that polite people don't talk about!"

"But wait!" Money starts to burst in.

"Let me finish," I say. "For example, I can remember about ten years ago, my father told me that he had made a will leaving my siblings and me and his wife equal shares in his estate. And the first thing that ran through my mind was, 'OK, so when are you going to die?'

"Whoa! Who thought that? Was it me? Yes. Isn't that crude?" Money nods. "Isn't it almost like *bathroom* talk to speak of these things?" Money nods.

"Even so, that's what you did to me. Once, when I was in the Ft. Lauderdale church, an elderly parishioner came to me to tell me that she was leaving a lot of you to the church. I swear, I began to salivate. I hate that! Do you see how powerful you are? You can make me salivate when all I want to do is be a loving minister. I am terrified that someone is going to see me looking at them with 'tombstone eyes.'"

"So what do you do?" asks Money.

Is he making fun of me? I hold myself up. I say, "I have simply learned to ignore my drool and get on with being a minister or a son." I then rush to wrap up my thoughts. "So there it is. You, Money, are this powerful reality that connects us to our own fear and greed, and either pushes us around or draws us on in the service of material egoism."

Money stares at me. "Are you finished?"

"Well, yeah," I say.

"You know, you got me all wrong," says Money. "Do you remember the first rule of the universe?"

I ponder that for a moment. "You mean the 'I have a problem and it's your fault' rule?"

Money nods. "You are dumping all your stuff on me and then making me responsible for it. Let me tell you the real story."

Chastised, I nod.

Money starts. "I am actually divine," it says. "I did not begin in selfishness or greed. I began in heaven. Of course, I'm not being literal here. It's just that I began as a divine *language* of sorts. In early hunting and gathering societies, I was a metaphor for the divine ability to valuate something. I could be salt, cattle, fish, shells, jewelry, glass beads, feathers, gold, or even human skulls. It didn't matter, really, for these things had been designated in some divine way as representing units of divine value. I was used ceremoniously to bestow prestige, settle psychic or material debts, to placate enemies and so on. I was seen as a divine valuation. This value was seen to be intangible manna or god-stuff, now made tangible in the form of a shell or a skull, which then *literally held the early culture together*. I was seen and valued as being a divine glue, a form of special communication, that held culture together by linking people together. Given this understanding, I was most appropriately controlled by priests and shamans, for in tradition-al societies, there was great emphasis put on balance and order in a tribe or a community. While ancient priests and shamans didn't have me, they were responsible for the proper *circulation* of me in the community. Through my circulation, social bonds and order were maintained.

"The point is that we can see that from earliest times, I was used as a kind of divine language—tangible and concrete words or symbols that communicated value. In ancient Rome, there was a temple dedicated to me. It was called the Temple of Juno Moneta. Moneta is the Roman version of the Greek goddess Mnemosyne, who was the goddess of memory. Memory, to the ancient Greeks and Romans, was the key to being human; it was the true gift of the gods. It is memory that allows us to accumulate experience and to assign it meaning and measure. Memory was to the Greeks what the Tree of Knowledge was to the Hebrews. So I was a form of cul-tural memory, just like language. Just as words stand for ideas and are exchanged in your communication, so do I stand for value, and I am also used in your communication.

"Money was the language of the gods translated into earthly terms. With money, you people can become like the gods. For example, Zeus can value Hercules, and he can translate that valu-ing into reality. Zeus can snap his fingers and, poof, Hercules now lives on Mt. Olympus. Likewise, you can value your daughter and translate that into reality. You can use money to put her, poof, not on Mt. Olympus, but on a college campus. St. Peter can declare the value of a soul at the gates of heaven and thus make it so. You can declare the value of your daughter's education and, with money, make it so. Gods speak the value of things, and they come to be the elements communicated into the realm of earthly reality. I am like this. By me, value is uttered and thus made real.

"So, in my inception, I am not this demonic root of all evil, but rather a marvelous invention which, like language, has allowed you people to evolve and grow and communicate in a world of symbols, where you can do more than just talk about what something means to you; you can make that meaning tangible. Money can materially, tangibly, say all sorts of things. I can say how valuable art is, or how valuable food is, or how much your family is worth to you, or how much your church is worth to you, or how much your denomination is worth to you.

"Now, it's important to remember that I am not the same as family, art, food, or your church, but I can concretely speak of value. I remain a symbol, but I am a tangible symbol. There's child money, parent money, retirement money, you and your partner are going to spend the rest of your lives together money, you don't want the people in West Africa to starve money. In each of these cases, I function as the tangible representation of a value. With me, you people can truly communicate because you can put your money where your mouths are. Without money, you would be just talk."

Money sits back, obviously proud of itself, gloating.

"But what about all that bad stuff I was talking about earlier?" I say.

Money steps back in. "I am a language," it says. "The question for you is: What do you want to say with me? It's not always easy to know if you are speaking the best values you can with money. What's important is to remember that you are speaking a value of some sort, even if it is only of ego. I am a language of value, and what do you want to say? Of course, I realize it's hard to think of me in these terms in a society such as yours, where I am often seen as my own reward. Still, you need to do it if I am going to fulfill my purpose. You need to give me my *spiritual* due."

"It's just so hard for me to think of you in those terms—you know, spiritually," I say.

"You must," says Money. "But it really isn't so hard. For example, if you look at me, you will see the evidence of my origins."

I peer at the dollar bill.

"What does it say?" asks Money.

"In God we trust," I read. "I always thought that was just civil religion, a concession to theological and fiscal conservatives."

"Oh, it's more than just that," says Money. "It's an artifact from antiquity, a sign of my divine origins."

"But how did things get so screwed up?" I ask.

"You people started valuing the wrong things with me," says Money. "It happened like this. In truly ancient times, it was the job of priests, priestesses, and shamans to see to it that I circulated, which I was supposed to do, so as to hold culture and society together! I was like the divine blood that circulates through the body of a culture, keeping it healthy and integrated. If you circulate me within a culture, you cultivate its living power. However, if you hoard me, it creates a backlog. A blood clot of sorts develops. The body gets out of balance and ill. The shamans and priests were there to see to it that this didn't happen.

"However, all of this began to fall apart with the slow disappearance of the hunting and gathering societies. The more evolved culture became, the more backlogs began to develop. Things really got out of whack beginning with the state minting me. Secular rulers took an institutional tip from the priests and said basically, 'I am the gods' chosen ruler, and I am going to mint this money, put my name and God's name on it, and because of that, it will be worth more than just a piece of metal. It will be of God and thus will be infused with value.' So, people believed their rulers were representative of the divine, and they believed in me in this new way.

"However, when the control of me passed from the sacred to the secular rulers, the safeguards of the past were left behind. Rulers were concerned not with maintaining a balance of wealth within society but rather with accumulating wealth. They wanted more wealth and power for themselves. Rulers saw themselves not as the caretakers of wealth but as its owners. So I became progressively concentrated and log-jammed. Rulers would accumulate massive amounts of money, not to redistribute but usually to use to make war. This practice has been an historical precedent since Gilgamesh. It's sad that I am most often accumulated for war. This is true for many countries, as we have seen—for example, with both Russia and the United States.

"And it is also true for companies. Why does QVC or VIA-COM need to be so big and rich? Why does GE need to be so big and rich? So it can conquer RCA and destroy it. Does it matter that a local economy is wounded and hundreds put out of work and that I am kept from doing my divine duty? No. You see, you people simply got trapped saying all the wrong things with me.

"Yet this approach is so strange to me, because I will only have value as long as I have a communal context. When the social bond breaks, the illusion falls, for the people will no longer believe in the divinity of money, or rather, they will no longer believe in my ability to hold society together as a literal language of value.

"It is only when you have an appropriate attitude toward me that I am allowed to do my job, which is to connect you all through communication. I must circulate! But how? Careless spending feeds only what is base in yourselves and in others. Rather, you should ask if your wealth serves what is above or below. Does it serve God? Does it serve the evolution of what is best in you? Or does it serve Mammon, the material ego? Does it serve compassion? Love? Does it serve any kind of value other than self?

"Do you know that when you feed the hungry, you feed God, you feed the growing edge of your own soul? You find God in those you clothe and feed. When you think of money as alms given to support your highest and not your lowest values, money changes character. It fulfills itself. It becomes a language of true value rather than of ego. Take yourself, for example."

"What?" I say, suddenly cautious.

"Your church gives me to you," says Money.

"There's nothing high falutin' about that," I say. "It's my *salary*. You know, an exchange of goods for services."

"Oh, poof," says Money. "You offer the gift of your being, all of who you are, and in return you are offered the gift of support. The church supports you and your family. This is not an exchange of goods for services; it is an exchange of values. When you are paid, I speak unfettered from any ego. Your pay check is a holy thing."

"Now wait a minute," I say. "We'll have none of that! This is a Unitarian church, not the Crystal Cathedral or the Swaggart Dome."

"So you are uncomfortable receiving *holy* money?" asks Money.

"I guess so," I say. "Yes, I am."

"Why?" says Money. "When I come into this place, I am made holy. I am spoken out of the highest ideals. When I am sent to support this Association of churches, it is the same. Since ancient times, one of the ways to give me my spiritual due has been to tithe. This is not the same as trying to buy off the universe. The Biblical tithe is one tenth of one's possessions. The Bible tells us that the ancient Hebrews tithed with great joy. Why this joy? Because when alms are dedicated to that which is highest within yourselves, you do rejoice, for you have spoken great poetry. To the early Hebrew, the temple was an outward manifestation of the highest inner reality. The same is true of your church and your denomination. Since ancient times, people have willingly given me up to bejewel a cross when they were destitute. They were not simply being fools. They were trying to *say something* with me! These kinds of people recognize that there are material underpinnings to the spiritual search. The pulpit isn't gold-plated, but the money in the collection plates still speaks."

"What do you mean?" I say, feeling somewhat cynical. "What does it say, clinking about in the plates every week? Does it say, 'The church is a business; pay up on your pledge'? Does it say, 'The more you give, the more attention we pay to you'? Does it say, 'Drool, Kit, drool!'?"

Here, Money sighs, "Stop it! Why do you Unitarian Universalists doubt yourselves so much when you are so full of holiness? *You Unitarian Universalists are so afraid of holiness!* Stop it! You know what the money in the plate says. It says, 'We all walk our own paths in life, but we do not walk alone. We walk together.' It says, 'We believe in each other, and we believe that together we can create a safe place, a sacred place, where we can be who we really are and be empowered to become the most we can be.' It says, 'We believe that together we can save each other and that together we can save the world.' It says all that, and it says more. Kit, it says that you and your gifts are valued. It says that all the staff is valued. It says that the programs of this church and this denomination are valued. It says that the pain and joys of all these people are worth enfolding and holding in a collective health. It says that life isn't stupid or hopeless. It says so much. Kit, never doubt the holiness of your church or of your *religion.*"

Here, I am hanging my head. "But I still have to do my sermon, so what do I say about you to all my parishioners?"

Money begins to fade here, falling flat onto my wallet. "Thank them," Money whispers. "Thank them for letting me be my best. Thank them for all the good and wonderful things they say with me. Thank them for letting me be sacred."

And Money lies silent.

And so now the moment comes. Here I am. Can I do it? Can I not make a joke or pass it off or be flip? Can I say what needs to be said? Can I do it? Can I tell the real truth?

OK, here goes. This church, this Association, this *religion* is a sacred presence in this world. That's the truth. Your love, your time, your work, and your *money* make it all possible. That's the next truth.

And the last truth, the biggest truth? It is this. Thank you. Thank you for all the good and wonderful things you say with money. Thank you for making money *holy.* Thank you for the Unitarian Universalist Association. Thank you for this church.

Thank you very, very much.
  In a world without end, Amen.

~

Personal Reflection

Reflect on your relationship with money in the different stages of
your life. When was that relationship most difficult and why?
When was it most satisfying and why?

  What have you supported financially that has made you feel
you are supporting "the growing edge of your own soul"? Is there
any way to make that a standard for your priorities?

For the Congregation

1. What do you think Kit Howell means when he says that
   Unitarian Universalists are "afraid of holiness"? Is it true, in
   your experience?
2. According to Howell's historical sketch, how did money go
   from being holy to being dirty in our perception? Is there any
   way to transform the way we view money?

THEOLOGY OF MONEY
AND FAIR EXCHANGE

REV. KEITH KRON

Starr King School for the Ministry
Berkeley, California

A good theology of money, like any good theology, looks at what can be revealed beneath the surface of things. Keith Kron delves into the essential dynamic that lies under our use of money, the exchange of value. If we are to be in right relationship to money, says Kron, then money must not be the end in itself but rather the means of exchanging what is of greatest importance to us.

Kron makes the concept real through a wonderful story about his relationship with his grandmother and through the events of a favorite children's book. This use of stories points us in exactly the right direction, for in our experiences with other people we find the most important meaning of fair exchange.

Once we locate that personal meaning, we can, as Kron suggests, extend the concept to issues of justice in the world. As with all the most powerful theologies, Kron brings the personal and the political, the individual and the global, together in his call to support the work of our Unitarian Universalist congregations. It is up to the rest of us to weave the same connection in our lives. —S. M.

MY GRANDMOTHER and I have always had a special relationship. One of the first things I remember about her was receiving fifty cents in the mail for Christmas so that I could go out and buy something I wanted. I went to the store and looked. What I really wanted was a Charlie Brown coloring book and a box of crayons. I looked and looked at the price, but no matter how hard I looked, I didn't have enough money for both. So I thought about it. There was also a less expensive Batman coloring book that I could actually afford. I stood there and thought. Finally, I remembered that in the store, next to the box of eight crayons I wanted, there was a smaller box of six crayons. I rushed back and took another look. Sure enough, this box was cheaper than the larger one. As I figured it out in my head, I realized that I had enough money to get that Charlie Brown coloring book and the box of six crayons.

That's not the most important part of the story. What remains vivid is the vision of sitting at the kitchen table and coloring a picture of Charlie Brown and his kite being eaten up by the kite-eating tree; I remember using those six crayons, being very happy with them, and thinking about how much I wanted to send this picture to my grandmother. I also recall getting an envelope and a stamp from my mother, putting the picture into the envelope, and mailing it to my grandmother. I wasn't there when she opened it, but I know what the expression on her face was when she saw the drawing. I can always see her smiling, and I know both how important it was for her to get that picture and how important it was for me to send it.

I like this story because it is one example of the way my grandmother and I have always communicated very well. The reason that we communicate so well is that we both place a lot of value on our relationship. I have placed a lot of value on who she is, and she has placed a lot of value on me for being there.

We've always had a lot of different ways that we have communicated. Communicating by mail, as when I sent her the picture, is one example. Another method lies in the words that we spoke to each other whenever we were together. The conversations that we had were also an important way of communicating, as were the facial expressions, such as just looking up and smiling at one another. In fact, the knowing exchange of faces can tell so much, as can a touch—a hug, a kiss, sitting next to someone and having her arm around you and feeling good. When my grandfather died, I was the person who sat next to my grandmother; we didn't say anything or do anything, but we were communicating the entire time just by being present to one another.

This all speaks about paying attention. My grandmother and I paid attention to one another. Think about that phrase, *paying attention*. There is an exchange; something goes back and forth. An American businesswoman wrote, "Communication is a measurable asset." The attention that my grandmother and I paid to each other was a measurable asset.

These two quarters are another way of communicating, another measurable asset. You know that this fifty cents means much more than fifty cents. But let us look at where money has had a simple meaning, as we go back in time. Think about the possibility of what it was supposed to have been—a symbol, a communication between you and me, of a good and fair exchange.

We began with the trading of goods, and then we came up with the idea of money. Your goods were going to be traded for this money, and it was used as a tool for communication. The transaction was a sacred and holy one. If you look at our coins today, they still have religious words stamped right on them. They are a symbol of religious exchange, a way to communicate. That is very important as we look at the way we want to create meaning for money in our congregations and organizations.

A friend of mine told me that she considered me a great communicator. One of the things that I do very well, she said, is to communicate meaning and messages to others. And you know what? I never saw these coins as communication. I've always been very poor with money, I think because I never saw it as a way to communicate, and I've always done a very poor job of dealing with money, from balancing my checkbook to budgeting to knowing just what to do with it. I've looked at money wrongly all of my life, as so many of us have.

I'd like to share a story, probably my all-time favorite story. It's a parable of our time, and it's from the book *Maniac Magee*. I really want to use this story to help illustrate some of the points I am making. Just sit back and enjoy the magic of this piece of this story.

Maniac is a homeless child who has wandered into this neighborhood. At the corner drug store, there is a knot, called Cobble's Knot, which has never been untied by anyone. If the wonders of the world hadn't stopped at seven, Cobble's Knot would have been number eight.

Nobody knew how it got there. As the story goes, the original Mr. Cobble wasn't doing too well with the original Cobble's Corner Grocery at the corner of Hector and Birch. In his first two weeks, all he sold was some Quaker Oats and some penny candy.

> Then one morning, as he unlocked the front door for business, he saw the Knot. It was dangling from the flagpole that hung over the big picture window, the one that said FROST-ED FOODS in icy blue-and-white letters. He got out a pair of scissors and was about to snip it off, when he noticed what an unusual and incredible knot it was.
>
> Then he got an idea. He would offer a prize to anyone who could untangle the Knot. Publicize it. Call the newspaper. Winner's picture on the front page, Cobble's Corner in the background. Business would boom.
>
> Well, he went and did it, and if business didn't exactly boom, it must have peeped a little, because eons later, when Maniac Magee came to town, Cobble's Corner was still there. Only now it sold pizza instead of groceries. And the

prize was different. It had started out being sixty seconds alone with the candy counter; now it was one large pizza per week for a whole year.

In time, the prize made the Knot practically priceless. That is why, after leaving it outside for a year, Mr. Cobble took it down, kept it in a secret place inside the store, and brought it out only to meet a challenger.

If you look at old pictures in the Two Mills Times, you see that the Knot was about the size and shape of a lopsided volleyball. It was made out of string, but it had more contortions, ins and outs, twists and turns and dips and doodles than the brain of Albert Einstein himself. It had defeated all comers for years, including J.J. Thorndike, who grew up to be a magician, and Fingers Halloway, who grew up to be a pickpocket.

Hardly a week went by without somebody taking a shot at the knot, and losing. And each loser added to the glory that awaited someone who could untie it.

"So you see," said Amanda, "if you go up there and untie Cobble's Knot—which I know you can—you'll get your picture in the paper and you'll be the biggest hero ever around here and nooo-body'll mess with you then."

Maniac listened and thought about it and finally gave a little grin. "Maybe you're just after the pizza, since you know I can't eat it."

Amanda screeched. "Jeff-freee! The pizza's not the point." She started to hit him. He laughed and grabbed her wrists. And he said okay, he'd give it a try.

They brought out the Knot and hung it from the flagpole. They brought out the official square wooden table for the challenger to stand on, and from the moment Maniac climbed up, you could tell the knot was in big trouble.

To the ordinary person, Cobble's Knot was about as friendly as a nest of yellow jackets. Besides the tangle itself, there was the weathering of that first year, when the knot hung outside and became as hard as a rock. You could barely make out the individual strands. It was grimy, moldy, crusted over. Here and there a loop stuck out, maybe big enough to stick your pinky finger through, pitiful testimony to the challengers who had tried and failed.

And there stood Maniac, turning the knot, checking it out. Some say there was a faint grin on his face, kind of playful, as though the knot wasn't his enemy at all, but an old pal just playing a little trick on him. Others say his mouth was more grim than grin, that his eyes lit up like flashbulbs, because he knew he was finally facing a knot that would stand up and fight, a worthy opponent.

He lifted it in his hands to feel the weight of it. He touched here and there, gently, daintily. He scraped a patch of crust off with his fingernail. He laid his fingertips on it, as though feeling for a pulse.

Only a few people were watching at first, and half of them were Heck's Angels, a roving tricycle gang of four and five-year-olds. Most of them had had sneaker-lace or yo-yo knots untied by Maniac, and they expected this would only take a couple of seconds longer. When the seconds became minutes, they started to get antsy, and before ten minutes had passed, they were zooming off in search of somebody to terrorize.

The rest of the spectators watched Maniac poke and tug and pick at the knot. Never a big pull or yank, just his fingertips touching and grazing and peck-pecking away, like some little bird.

"What's he doin'?" somebody said.

"What's taking so long?"

"He gonna do it or not?"

After an hour, except for a few more finger-sized loops, all Maniac had to show for his trouble were the flakes of knot crust that covered the table.

"He ain't even found the end of the string yet," somebody grumbled, and almost everybody but Amanda took off. Maniac never noticed. He just went on working.

By lunchtime, they were all back, and more kept coming. Not only kids, but grownups too, black and white, because Cobble's Corner was on Hector, and the word was racing through the neighborhoods on both the east and west sides of the street.

What people saw they didn't believe.

The knot has grown, swelled, exploded. It was a frizzy globe—the newspaper the next day described it as a "gigantic hairball." Now, except for a packed-in clump at the center, it was practically all loops. You could look through it and see Maniac calmly working in the other side.

"He found the end!" somebody gasped, and the corner burst into applause.

Meanwhile, inside, Cobble's was selling pizza left and right, not to mention zeps (a Two Mills type of hoagie), steak sandwiches, strombolis, and gallons of soda. Mr. Cobble himself came out to offer Maniac some pizza, which Maniac of course politely turned down. He did accept an orange soda, though, and then a little kid, whose sneaker laces Maniac had untied many a time, handed up to him a three-pack of Tastykake butterscotch Krimpets.

After polishing off the Krimpets, Maniac did the last thing anybody expected: he lay down and took a nap right there on the table, the knot hanging above him like a hairy planet, the mob buzzing all around him. Maniac knew what the rest of them didn't: the hardest part was yet to come. He had to find the right routes to untangle the mess, or it would just close up again like a rock and probably stay that way forever. He would need the touch of a surgeon, the alertness of an owl, the cunning of three foxes, and the foresight of a grand master in chess. To accomplish that, he needed to clear his head, to flush away all distraction, especially the memory of the butterscotch Krimpets, which had already hooked him.

In exactly fifteen minutes, he woke up and started back in.

Like some fairy tale tailor, he threaded the end through the maze, dipping and doodling through the openings the way he squiggled a football through a defense. As the long August afternoon boiled along, the exploded knot-hairball would cave in here, cave in there. It got lumpy, out of shape, saggy. The Times photographer made starbursts with his camera. The people munched on Cobble's pizza and spilled across Hector from sidewalk to sidewalk to sidewalk and said, "Ouuuu! and Ahhhh!"

And then, around dinnertime, a huge roar went up, a volcano of cheers: Cobble's Knot was dead. Undone. Gone. It was nothing but string.

I think of this story, which is really a parable, and I think of the knot we've tied tightly around money in our lives. It seems impossible to unravel, and it raises the question, "Why bother even untying it?" My answer to the question is simple: We have to look at what's really there. When we untie the knot, we're left with string. We can see the string not as a knot but as a tool, something that we can use.

Also, I resonate with the part of the story in which Maniac figures out what the problem is, and the hardest part is yet to come. In other words, we've identified the problem, but how do we solve it?

I think of these two quarters and my grandmother, and what I really remember is the fact that these two quarters weren't important. The fact that my grandmother wanted me to have something and that she loved me, and that I loved her enough to get the coloring book and send the picture to her was an example of fair exchange. She and I exchanged love for each other; the coins were just the tool. This was not the end but rather the means by which the important exchange happened.

In our religious association, in the Unitarian Universalist Association, this is exactly the right time for us to be examining the concept of fair exchange. You look at all of the work we have just started doing toward racial justice in our Association; it is about nothing more than setting up a fair exchange between people. Sexism, homophobia, heterosexism, racism, classism—working on all these problems goes back to setting up a fair exchange between people and putting ourselves back in equal, right relationship.

Thomas Starr King, for whom my alma mater is named, described money and how it is used: "All our money has a moral stamp. It is coined over again in an inward mint. The uses we put it to, the spirit in which we spend it, give it a character which is plainly perceptible to the eye of God." We want to put the spirit and the moral stamp back in our money and use it as a tool.

Theologian and money expert Jacob Needleman says we have to pay more attention to money, not less. We can't pretend that it's going to go away. We must put our Unitarian Universalist moral stamp on it.

Take a look at what's happening in the world today. What is the number one thing that's traded and sold more than anything else? It's not goods. It's not things. It's money—people trading currencies. What does that say about a moral stamp? People are trading money to get more money. I don't understand. Instead, we should be valuing people and their actions and using this fifty cents as the tool, as the exchange.

I think about a major gift that someone may give to a congregation, and I think about the Charlie Brown picture that I sent to my grandmother. What both clearly represent is a fair exchange. Something has been done that is a fair exchange for something about to be done. A person who gives a major gift to a congregation has been enriched by that congregation; the life of the church is important to that person, whoever she or he might be. Similarly, when my grandmother got the Charlie Brown picture, she knew that I valued her and she valued me. Both of these are examples of money as the means to value people rather than an end in itself. They are examples of the fair exchange, of paying attention to that which we value. They are about sending the message that we value and honor the inherent worth and dignity of every person.

When we untie the knot and we get string, we see a tool to connect things fairly. When we untie the knot of money, we can see it for what it is—a communications symbol and a tool that should represent the fair exchange. The people involved have their inherent worth and dignity.

That is what we, as Unitarian Universalists, value.

∾

Personal Reflection

Who in your life has taught you the deeper meaning of "fair exchange"? What was exchanged, and what were the symbols of its value?

For the Congregation

1. If money is a communication tool, what is communicated in your congregation when you discuss and use money? What do you communicate to your larger community?
2. Is money a knot in your congregation? If so, why? What would it take to untangle the knot and treat money as a tool to represent free exchange and communicate your deepest values?
3. Do you agree with Thomas Starr King that "all money has a moral stamp"? If so, what stamp would you like put on the money your congregation raises and spends?

BANKING ON A DREAM

REV. GARY E. SMITH
First Parish
Concord, Massachusetts

Gary Smith reminds his congregation of something we must always remember when we decide how well we will support our churches. Simply put, we live on the commitments, or as Smith would say, the investments and the dreams, of those who came before us. This fact is of vital importance because it reveals to us the short-sightedness of approaching our churches as consumers who will pay for what we get. In a sense, what history really calls us to do is to pay for what we give.

Smith's sermon indirectly reminds us that the real rewards will not be reaped in the coming year alone. We see long-term benefits of our time and resources in other areas of life, as well. We know a teacher's investment of time and caring will pay off in the development of students' minds and talents. We know the energy given to a cause we believe in will come to fruition some day down the road, when the cause is won, even if by others. So it is with the most profound rewards that grow from the gifts we make in religious community. They will be reaped some other time, just as we reap the gifts of those who came before us. Smith explains why supporting our church is not a matter of giving something away, but rather of investing in what we might all earn together. —S. M.

I AM TOLD that this past Tuesday, as the hour for the drawing of
the $28-million Mass Millions Lottery was getting closer, that
tickets were sold at the rate of 250 thousand every fifteen minutes.
Talk about "banking on a dream." This is a sermon about banking
on a dream, but I'll get to that in a moment.

I've thought about the lottery this week. I really don't like it,
and in my own silent protest, I've never purchased a ticket. All the
advertising and promotions prey upon those who can least afford
to gamble, encouraging them to take their milk money, come up
with a sequence of six or seven numbers, and hope for the best
against astronomically high odds. But I won't be able to convince
that winning family down on the Cape of my argument. The husband is unemployed, living year-round in what I take to be a summer cottage with three young children, supported by his wife's
part-time work at a Stop and Shop, he takes ten dollars he surely
could have used for something else, and *bang*, he will be drawing
an $870-thousand check for each of the next twenty years.

There is something very, very strange about a population that
is quite willing to let health care costs go through the roof and let
the education of our children go down the tubes, a population
that is willing to witness a growing number of children sleeping
on the streets or in welfare motel rooms, a population that will
passively drive along as chunks of concrete fall from bridge over-
passes, and yet will line up like cattle to buy lottery tickets at a rate
of 277 tickets a second. What kind of a dream does this population bank on? God forbid we should make anyone accountable
for how our tax dollars should be spent. Instead, we let the
Congress fuss about child care for the attorney general, and we let
our state government take two weeks to find a way to let some
developers rip us off in the building of a new Boston Garden.
What if we ever got around to talking about real things, like common dreams?

We are still caught in a mode of banking on the dream of the
1980s—what's in it for *me*? Forget *your* dream, we say. Forget *our*

dreams, our common dreams. That lottery ticket has everything to do with *my* dream. The dream of the 1980s finds its metaphor in something like the savings and loan scandals: How can I take money to make money? Frederick Buechner is absolutely right: "You can be a millionaire one moment and a pauper the next without lifting a finger. Great fortunes can be made and lost completely on paper. There is," he says, "more concrete reality in a baby throwing its rattle out of a crib."

If we took the sum total invested in lottery tickets in this country; added the amount spent on point spreads for your next local, friendly college basketball game; took the Bingo receipts out of Ledyard, Connecticut, where they can't build hotel rooms for the players fast enough; took all these dollars, which are nothing more than a scheme and a prayer to *please make me rich*; if we took these dollars, the sum of which would scare you to death, and thought about putting them into common dreams like getting people into homes and food into stomachs, and insisting that education matters in this country and that health care can really make sense—in other words, if we could bring our dreams together, we could change this world. This is a sermon about common dreams. We should be sick and tired of any attitude that smacks of "What's in it for me?"

This is a sermon about banking on a dream, and by now you know that I'm not talking about just your dream or my dream; I'm talking about the dreams we have in common right here in this place. If, here at First Parish, we can practice prying our fingers apart and letting go of a little bit of what we have so that all can share in the dream, maybe the idea of common dreaming will become infectious and spill over into civil government.

"Banking on a Dream," the Fundraising Committee said to me, "that's your sermon theme for this year." Whoever thought the sermon would begin with a lottery drawing, this notion that the right combination of numbered ping-pong balls can put you on Easy Street? I am asking you to bank on a dream today that has everything to do with all of us together. Let's get out of the way right now the conflict of interest in my remarks: Of course, part of this budget pays my salary. I know that, but they asked me to speak anyway. It also provides the salaries of some very talented people here who work hard on your behalf, and believe me, none of us went into this business for the money.

This budget belongs to you *and* to me—religious education, music, social justice, buildings and grounds, wider denomination, youth ministry, adult programs, social gatherings. And by the way, thanks to those who had the courage here, some years ago, to hold up 2½ percent as a guideline for giving. If it has started you thinking, that is entirely the point. We don't want to talk about whether it means 2½ percent of gross or net income. We don't want to talk about college tuitions or fixed incomes. None of that matters. It's entirely up to you. You decide.

But I'll say this. If you make a six-figure income and head off to Aruba three times a year, and then you feel good about dropping five bucks in the plate each week, small blessings on you. And if you have nothing and are nursing a loved one back to health with little insurance and have to plan grocery purchases one day to the next, and you put five bucks in the plate each week, great blessings upon you. I think that is what 2½ percent is all about.

For those of you who are keeping track, I'm about halfway there. Now, I want to say some words about First Parish, who we have been and who we are and who we might become; I want to say some words about First Parish in the context of common dreams. It strikes me that if you took our written history, *The Meeting House on the Green*, and just opened it randomly, here and there, you'd find nothing but a story of common dreams.

Consider those eleven people who ventured out here from Cambridge in 1635 to make Concord the first inland European settlement on the North Atlantic coast. Those must have been days of common, selfless dreams, days of building a meeting house, forming a community, one for all, all for one. Of course, I don't think the 2½-percent "donation" was voluntary in the seventeenth century, but these were folks fresh from a religious persecution that must have left them gasping for the air of freedom. They were content to find common cause in the kind of mutual support that would let them hear the uninhibited truth spoken from a pulpit like this. I have to think that, in those days, a common dream was essential for survival.

In the eighteenth century, Concord brought "the rude bridge that arched the flood," and who can begin to imagine what this First Parish must have been in those days leading up to the Revolution, here under the ministry of William Emerson (grandfather of you-know-who)? There can there be no doubt at all that it was a time of common dreams, here in the midst of a new nation, one for all and all for one. John Teele says that William Emerson was a fiery patriot who "used his pulpit to make his political convictions as a citizen clearly known."

And then Teele cites George Tolman, who notes that "sixty men enlisted in the Minutemen following a sermon which Emerson preached from Psalm 113," though he also writes that "though there seemed to be no connection between the Psalm and going off to war . . . these men seemed to get the idea anyway and joined up." Common dreams. Banking on a dream even.

And the nineteenth century? We could speak of the beginning of American Unitarianism and this church's role in its development—common dreams indeed. But I like Dana Greeley's observation that "the spirit of Concord" itself was born in this century at the height of the abolitionist movement, the Civil War, the reconstruction. The church in these days, Dana said, "became as strong as it has ever been." One hymn I like to sing is "O God of Earth and Altar," which expresses the prayerful state of our condition in this or any century. "Our people drift and die," we sing. There was little drifting in the late nineteenth century. This country and this town were reeling from the shock of a time when all might have been lost, and this church, this First Parish, flourished in its common life. Banking on a dream. The dream lived on 250 years later.

And then, at the very dawning of the twentieth century, in 1901, this building burned to the ground, and those who came before us needed dreams again for the rebirth and rebuilding. Rebuild they did, and Samuel Eliot, president of the American Unitarian Association, preached here for the occasion. "The power . . . of this institution," he said, "can justly be measured by the union and proportion of its sense of continuity and its sense of a new beginning. . . . There are here the abundant evidences alike of stability and of movement, of permanence and elasticity." This century began with dreaming, and how shall it end?

And what of First Parish and the twenty-first century? Are we still capable of coming together in common purpose? What would we look like if we banked on our dream? If your family is like my own, you invest and bank on many dreams—putting money aside for college tuition, money aside for retirement, money aside for mortgage and food, some money perhaps even set aside for vacations. As families, as individuals, we bank, we save, we invest, and today we ask your consideration for First Parish as a place to also invest in your dreams. Consider this sermon as a prospectus. I believe the dividends are considerable.

"Saddle your dreams before you ride them," said Howard Thurman. And that is our task this week; annual fund raising is a time to get down to business, to saddle dreams, to come up against what Thurman called "the hard facts of the world before we [can] ride them off among the stars." Who knows what this coming year will bring, what these later years of the twentieth century will bring, what the dawning of the new century to come will bring? Perhaps you will be investing in your children's future. Perhaps you win by investing in your own.

First Parish has been here, not on Easy Street but on Lexington Road, for nearly eighteen generations, a legacy of men and women who have found common purpose in their dreams, eighteen generations of men and women who *have* banked on their dreams. Make no mistake about it, we are their beneficiaries. "[Dreams] become for us the bearers of the new possibility," Howard Thurman concluded, "the enlarged horizon, the great hope. Even as they romp among the stars they come back to their place in our lives, bringing with them the radiance of the far heights, the lofty regions, and giving to all our days the lift and the magic of the stars." I ask you today to give your own magic to the stars.

∼

Personal Reflection

Are you investing your resources—your time, your energy, your love, your money—in those things that are likely to last the ages? What changes, if any, would you like to make in your most fundamental investments?

For the Congregation

1. Take a careful look at the history of your congregation. What remarkable investments did your forebears make in the future of free religion? What were the obstacles they had to overcome in order to "bank on" this relatively unknown body of thought and deed? Are you living up to their dreams? How or how not?

2. What do you think future members of your church will say about your investments? What will they think you have banked on?

THE JINGLE OF COINS

REV. GARY E. SMITH
First Parish
Concord, Massachusetts

Gary Smith challenges a critical assumption when he questions our tendency to talk about our pledges to our congregations as being one among other charitable contributions. Sometimes we even claim that we do not give more as Unitarian Universalists because we give so much to other causes. We are stingy with our churches, so the logic goes, because we are such generous people!

As Smith points out, there is, or there should be, something different in our financial commitments to our religious communities. They grow out of a sacred search for our highest aspirations, and they represent our deepest values; as such they become a vital piece of our existence in the world. Perhaps the other causes we believe in should encourage us to give more to our Unitarian Universalist congregations, which work to make sure there will always be a role for reformers in the world.

It is tempting to stand at the back of the sanctuary, observing, holding back, slipping a dollar into the plate, perhaps sticking a hand into a pocket and jingling the loose coins there. Think twice, though. The experience is so much better from the front. –S. M.

FROM TIME TO TIME, whenever the Cadi who governed the village and gave judgments in the court was absent, the role was given to the Hodja (a Holy One). It was under just such circumstances that, one day, an unusual and difficult case was presented to the court. A local innkeeper brought suit against a poor student in these terms:

"He has lingered outside my restaurant, Holy One, and thus has stolen from me."

"And what has he stolen?" inquired the Hodja.   .

"The good smell of my good food," replied the innkeeper. "Unwilling to pay for the food itself, he has lingered around the door of my kitchen daily and availed himself of what was not his, the aromas of my cooking. Thus, I work and slave, and this scoundrel takes advantage of my labors and will not pay."

"Is this true, young man?" the Hodja demanded.

"It is, Holy One. I am a poor student, scarcely able to pay for my room and my books. I live on scraps, which I beg wherever I can. But the wonderful smells from the inn I could not resist, and so daily I hang about the kitchen and imbibe those odors, and thus imagine that I am eating those very delicacies."

"And have you any money on you now?" asked the Hodja.

"Only a few coppers, Holy One," was the reply.

"Hand them over."

As the poor student passed his last coins to the Hodja, the innkeeper smiled with satisfaction. The Hodja turned to him then and said, "Innkeeper, close your eyes, and listen well to my judgment."

Puzzled, the innkeeper did so. And then, with his eyes tightly shut, he heard the student's coins being jingled in the Hodja's hand.

"Do you hear, innkeeper?" asked the Hodja.

"I hear, wise one," replied the innkeeper.

"Good! The sound of the coins has paid for the smell of the food," replied the Hodja, as he returned the coins to the student.

This is a Middle Eastern story about payment in kind, and this is also a sermon about payment in kind. This is the time of year when those of us in the free churches have to admit, after all, that there is very little that is free about a free church except our freedom. You have watched with me for these past several weeks as the wonderful series of order of service inserts and newsletter articles have spoken of the ways in which we, as a community of faith, have tried to respond to one another and to this world in this past year. We are now asking for payment in kind. If you have experienced something here beyond the smell, we are asking you for more than the jingle.

The experience in Romania within the Unitarian congregations of Transylvania brings home, in very powerful ways, the importance of what we do here today. These congregations, as with all other recognized state churches of Romania, under both the old regime of Ceausescu and under the new, are fully supported by the state through taxes. But *fully supported* is not exactly the way to put it. For if your hymnbooks are paid for by the state, and your buildings are maintained by the state, and your clergy are both educated and supported by the state, nothing is free.

However, if your congregation wanted more hymnbooks or different hymnbooks or new hymnbooks, if your congregation wanted to build a new building or start a new congregation across town, if you wanted your son or daughter to study for the ministry, if you were a member of the clergy speaking out against the government, then nothing would be free. No new books could be printed, no new churches could be built, theological schools would be severely limited, and free-speaking clergy would be reassigned to distant parishes. That is the meaning of a state church.

Our spiritual forebears in Transylvania, England, and Europe knew these restrictive meanings. Part of our role in the Reformation, and subsequently in the emergence of the American church, was directed to establishing the fundamental place of freedom of religion and the privilege to support our chosen community of faith voluntarily. This is the day to renew that privilege. This is the day to say that if you are participating here in ways that move you beyond merely catching the smells from outside that door, we are hoping to receive more than the jingle of your coins. That is my first point, that what we do here today has something to do with payment in kind and celebrates the heritage of freedom which separates the support of the church from the taxes of the state (thank God). But if we are not supported by the state through our taxes, how do we determine and classify the kind of payment we then make here in the form of a pledge? The Internal Revenue Service classifies your gifts under charitable deductions, and I had thought for a long time that this was what my pledge payment to the church was—a donation, a charity, a payment to be lumped with my gifts to the university and the Heart Fund and to Public Radio. And although when we list all these donations together on Schedule A of Form 1040, we are lumping these gifts together and calculating whatever percentage it is that we give away, I think we put the wrong emphasis on what we are doing.

Point number two, we are not a charity. This congregation may be a 501c3 or whatever the classification is that bestows a tax-free status upon us, but we are not a charity. Strictly speaking, we do help the needy, but more often than not, we are the needy ones. Please tell me that there is something measurably different for you in the giving and in the receiving here than there is in the dropping off of your old sweater in the Morgan Memorial truck at Stop and Shop. We are not a charity.

John Wolf, the minister of All Souls Unitarian Church in Tulsa, once cataloged for his congregation some reasons for supporting a Unitarian Universalist church. "You *want* to support it because it stands against superstition and fear. Because it points to what is noblest and best in human life. Because it is open to men and women of whatever race, creed, color, or place of origin.

You want to support it because it has a free pulpit. Because you can hear ideas expressed there which could cost any other minister his or her job. You want to support it because it is a place where children can come without being saddled with guilt or terrified of some celestial Peeping Tom, where they can learn that religion is for joy, for comfort, for gratitude and love.

You want to support it because it is a place where walls between people are torn down rather than built up. Because it is a place for the religious, displaced persons of our time, the refugees from mixed marriages, the unwanted free thinkers, and those who insist against orthodoxy that they must work out their own beliefs.

You want to support a Unitarian Universalist church because it is more concerned with human beings than with dogmas. Because it searches for the holy, rather than dwelling upon the depraved. Because it calls no one a sinner, yet knows how deep is the struggle in each person's breast and how great is the hunger for what is good.

You want to support a Unitarian Universalist church because it can laugh. . . . You want to support it because it insults neither your intelligence nor your conscience, and because it calls you to worship what is truly worthy of your sacrifice.

If these words of John Wolf capture at all why it is that you have joined this church, then are these not also the reasons for your support? And if you have experienced more than the whiff of these things from outside the door, then are these not worthy of more than the jingle of your coins? When I use the story of the student and the innkeeper to speak of payment in kind, I am not speaking of charity. I am not speaking of whatever the transaction is when you write a check to your college alumni fund, though there may be a value there in what you received from that college in years past. I am not speaking of the dynamic that happens when you drop a coin into the Salvation Army bucket at the holidays, whatever that is for you, or however good that might make you feel.

When you signed the membership book here, I hope that commitment took your measure of support to a different level, transformed this into some sense of belonging, an integration that moves beyond the dues to the health club or the golf club or the ownership of a ski condo and begins to speak of associating this place with your own values. And this leads me now to my third and final point: If your signing of a pledge form this afternoon is not the same as noting a tax deduction on your paycheck stub, and if it is something measurably different from the alphabet of charitable contributions we all make, then may I suggest that the money represented behind the dollar amounts you put on a pledge form stands for something, stands as a symbol for what you value.

"Money is the yardstick of value in the exchange of one thing for another," writes David Appelbaum in a recent issue of the excellent magazine *Parabola*. "It belongs to the class of great mental inventions known as measures. Mind, memory and money all derive from the Indo-European root word 'me' or 'men,' meaning 'to measure.' Measure fixes limits, degrees, amounts and quantities. Money brings things of different value together without becoming one or the other."

Money is a measure. Money stands for something. Money is a symbol for what we value. We spend money for our survival, certainly—our homes, our food, our clothing. We spend money for transportation, for education, for entertainment. We spend money for vacations. To peek into any of our checkbooks is to see there, first-hand, what we value. We're all different; we all have different financial situations. Some of us have little discretionary income; some of us have a great deal.

"Money," says Will Saunders, "is the way in which we express our aspirations, our dreams, our beliefs, our ideals. Money can be used to build up or to tear down, to serve or to dominate, to liberate or to oppress." When we speak of this church as a place worthy of support, when we speak of this church as a place where your religious faith and mine can come to find expression, when we speak of this church as a place that has been maintained for generations so that you and I can have it here for us in our own day, then we begin to come close to what your support means—not a tax, not a charity, but an expression of your values.

Fundamentally, we are asking for payment in kind, payment to yourself really, and in support of your beliefs, we are asking for your willingness to allocate some of your resources to support what you stand for. You are those who have said that you wish to belong; you are not hovering about the door, catching only the hint of what's cooking inside. You have tasted what we have to offer and now we seek from you the resources to move ahead, making this community of faith available to others, just as it was here for us when we needed it.

"The jingle of coins," writes Ellen Draper, "evokes both our basest attitudes and our highest aspirations." May the jingle of coins today be more than a sound only, and together may we find our highest aspirations in this place, this place we call sacred, this blessed community of seekers and doers.

~

Personal Reflection

Is it ever okay just to observe rather than participate, in other words, to "jingle the coins in your pocket"? In which arenas of your life do you find yourself taking that role? If you could move to what Gary Smith calls "payment in kind" in just one of those arenas, which would it be? What would be required?

For the Congregation

1. When we are frustrated with giving levels in our congregations, or perhaps simply searching for a new approach to stewardship, we sometimes fantasize about charging dues or fees for services. Is that kind of system what Gary Smith means by "payment in kind"?

2. If you were on the Stewardship Committee of your church and you were charged to write a brochure explaining what it means to make "payment in kind," what would you say?

3. The church, Smith writes, is "not a tax, not a charity, but an expression of your values." Which of your values are expressed in and by your congregation? Make a communal list. Are these values expressed in your efforts to raise money among your members? How might they take a more central role in education and solicitation?

THE GIFT MUST ALWAYS MOVE:
A THEOLOGY OF GIVING

REV. STEPHEN D. EDINGTON
Unitarian Universalist Church
Nashua, New Hampshire

Lewis Hyde's explanation of the Native American notion of "keeping the gift moving" has been a significant gift, in itself, to those of us seeking to weave together theologies of giving for ourselves and the congregations we serve. Here, Steve Edington connects Hyde's idea, in a cogent and heartfelt sermon, to the task of fundraising in our congregations and to the deeper reasons that the task matters.

Edington's own experience as a child committed to supporting and improving the traditional religious community of which he was a part challenges us to do as well in our liberal religious communities. The chance to be part of a meaningful and growing enterprise provided him an opportunity for learning and personal growth. Can we keep the gift moving in our own congregations? Edington makes the case.

Most importantly, Edington asserts that while the techniques and practical considerations of fundraising remain important, the deeper connection, the answer to the question "Why?" is even more essential. We need, he says, to be able to answer the question, "Why do we care for and about our liberal religious institutions in an ultimate sense?" When we can answer that, we will know what we are doing. —S. M.

WHEN THE PURITANS first landed in Massachusetts, they discovered a thing so curious about the Indians' feelings for property that they felt called upon to give it a name. In 1764, when Thomas Hutchinson wrote his history of the colony, the term was already an old saying: "An 'Indian gift,'" he told his readers, "is a proverbial expression signifying a present for which an equivalent return is expected." We still use this, of course, and in an even broader sense, calling that friend an *Indian giver* who is so uncivilized as to ask us to return a gift he has given.

Imagine a scene: An Englishman comes into an Indian lodge, and his hosts—wishing to make their guest feel welcome—ask him to share a pipe of tobacco. Carved from a soft red stone, the pipe itself is a peace offering that has traditionally circulated among the local tribes, staying in each lodge for a time but always given away again sooner or later. And so the Indians, as is only polite among their people, give the pipe to their guest when he leaves. The Englishman is tickled pink. What a nice thing to send back to the British Museum! He takes it home and sets it on the mantelpiece. A time passes and the leaders of a neighboring tribe come to visit the colonist's home. To his surprise he finds his guests have some expectation in regard to his pipe, and his translator finally explains to him that if he wishes to show his goodwill he should offer them a smoke and give them the pipe. In consternation, the Englishman invents a phrase to describe these people with such a limited sense of private property. The opposite of "Indian giver" would be something like "white man keeper" (or maybe "capitalist"), that is, a person whose instinct is to remove property from circulation, to put it in a warehouse or museum (or, more to the point for capitalism, to lay it aside to be used for production).

The Indian giver (or the original one, at any rate) understood a cardinal property of the gift: whatever we have been given is supposed to be given away again, not kept. Or, if it is kept, something of similar value should move on in its stead, the way a billiard ball may stop when it sends another scurrying across the felt, its momentum transferred. You may keep your Christmas present, but it ceases to be a gift in the true sense unless you have given something else away. As it is passed along, the gift may be given back to the original donor, but this is not essential.

In fact, it is better if the gift is not returned but is given instead to some new, third party. The only essential is this: *The gift must always move.* There are other forms of property that stand still, that mark a boundary or resist momentum, but the gift keeps going.

—Lewis Hyde

I still remember quite well the first pledge, or canvass campaign, in which I ever took part. I was all of thirteen years old. When my hometown southern West Virginia Baptist church conducted an "every member" canvass, they meant every member! Since I'd been baptized at the age of ten, I was included, not just as a pledger, but as a canvasser as well. My job in that particular campaign in 1958 was to canvass some of the other young people in the church's junior high group to get each of them to make a pledge for the upcoming church year. It was literally a nickel-and-dime effort. A dollar a week was not a bad allowance in those days, and ten cents a week represented a tithe, or 10 percent. This suggested share was derived from the twenty-eighth chapter of Genesis, in which Jacob promises Yahweh a one-tenth return of all the worldly blessings that Yahweh bestows upon him.

So, some three thousand years after this original pledge, there I was riding my bicycle around St. Albans, West Virginia, seeing how many dime-a-week pledges I could secure. I'm unable to recall now how successful I was. The church must have met or come close to its goal because it continued to survive and grow. I do remember being glad that my friends remained my friends even after I'd lightened their wallets to the tune of five or ten cents a week.

My recounting of such an episode could, I imagine, set off some liberal alarm bells and send a few Unitarian Universalist red flags flying. Isn't that terribly exploitive? Sending out kids barely in their teens to shake down the allowances of other kids for a pledge campaign and using a 10-percent figure based on some obscure Biblical reference. My answer, in a word, is no. That campaign gave me and my friends a sense of participation in a larger effort. The church, at that time, wasn't even ten years old and needed all the help it could get. But it also had a firm sense of its own mission, of who it was and where it wanted to go, and that sense was shared right down to its youngest members. While I'd been attending for several years, after that canvass drive it became *my church* in a way it had not been before. My friends and I now had our financial stake in it too. As for that Jacob and Yahweh deal, well that account conveyed the idea that we were involved in something that ultimately went beyond the mechanics and realities of a single pledge drive. What we were doing also had something to do with God, who was very real to all in that church.

Today, that church owns a goodly portion of the city block where it erected its first modest building over forty years ago. Part of its large physical plant now includes a gymnasium that houses various neighborhood recreational activities for kids who live nearby. Some of those whom I canvassed thirty years ago are still there making their pledges today. My own religious and spiritual journey has been one that has brought me to a personal standpoint where there is very, very little in the way of that Baptist church's program or theology to which I can relate. But I remain ever grateful for the lessons it taught me about institutional ownership and about the value of extending one's personal gifts beyond the bounds of the self.

Now, I find myself a part of a liberal religious association that

is asking for, and searching for, a theology of giving. It's an interesting choice of words, representing not just a reason or rationale
to contribute financially to the life of the Association and its
member societies but a theological undergirding that will provide
the motivation to do so. Usually, when talk or action in our
churches and fellowships and in our larger Association turns to
matters of money, it is cast in terms of how much is needed to do
what and how we're going to get it. Such talk and action, furthermore, are crucial to institutional survival, and there is no way I
would want to diminish their importance. A *theology* of giving,
however, both transcends and participates in such temporal concerns. Questions of theology deal with the big *Why*. It's not only
why do we need or want this or that program, or a new staff person, or better physical facilities, but *why* do we care about and for
our liberal religious institutions in an *ultimate* sense? Or, indeed,
do our caring and our giving even operate on that level?

In the setting where I was first introduced to the art and adven-
ture of pledging, the theology of giving was simple, straightforward, and right up front. It went like this: All of your worldly
possessions, to say nothing of your spiritual salvation, have come
from God. As agents of the Almighty, it is up to us to see that these
blessings continue to be bestowed, i. e., God's work must also be our
own. Then the bottom line. In order for such work to go forth, God
needs 10 percent of what you made this year, so fill out your pledge
card accordingly! This was then softened up a bit with a caveat that
God knows your financial needs and predicaments better than any
canvasser, and the Lord is also a God of love, mercy, and understanding who only expects you to do the best you can. After all,
Jacob probably had some rough years too.

Yes, yes, I know, Godly appeals like that when it comes to raising money can be used for all manner of human exploitation and
manipulation. To this day, it still saddens and disgusts me to think
of all the dollars from low and fixed-income sources that went
into the care and feeding of Jim Bakker's megalomania. So long as

money is raised for religious purposes, there will be charlatans around raking off what they can. Still, such troublesome realities as these should not prevent us from exploring our own theology of giving.

However difficult many of us, myself included, now find it to relate to both the language and the theology that guided my youthful efforts at pledging and canvassing, there was a principle there we would do well to take seriously. What was really being called for was the perpetuation of a gift that had come from a source greater than any one of us and that would continue to be bestowed beyond any of our lifetimes. Our fundraising efforts were, in an ultimate sense, our way of assuring the means by which these divine gifts were received; in other words, the church through which they were bestowed would be there both for us and for those who came after us. It was our way of making sure that the gift would always move.

This principle is my starting point in the search for a Unitarian Universalist theology of giving: The gift must always move. It's a principle that, as Lewis Hyde demonstrates, has long been present in Native American culture. I want to look at Hyde's illustration more closely just a bit later, but first let's consider the nature of the gift itself. We open our services at the Nashua Unitarian Universalist church with a simple chalice lighting ritual that sometimes includes the Reverend Margorie Montgomery's responsive reading: "Life is a gift for which we are grateful. We gather in community to celebrate the glories and the mysteries of this great gift." I'm aware that the expression "Life is a gift" can easily become terribly trivialized, right up there or down there with "Have a nice day." Seriously considered, however, it's a very profound affirmation.

It's an affirmation, for one thing, of human limitation. However much we religious liberals may celebrate the power of the human spirit, the reaches of the human mind, and the strength of the human will, the truth remains that we did not think, will, or spiritually generate ourselves into existence. (Sorry, Shirley MacLaine, but that's the way I see it!) We were given the life we have by a combination of forces with which we had nothing to do. That life is given to us is a biological and evolutionary reality; to choose to regard it as a gift, thereby implying a giver, however, is an affirmation of faith. It is an affirmation made in the face of all that might deny life's gift-like quality.

When Albert Camus, an individual whom I regard as a secular saint, pushed life to its extremities, he encountered what he called "The Absurd," the ultimate absurdity and meaninglessness of it all. And no one who lives life at any depth at all can escape his own periodic encounters with the absurd. But to remain open to all that life offers is also to encounter the gift, those moments when we experience, sometimes in the midst of pain and meaninglessness, the profound givenness of our existence.

In her moving and sometimes haunting book, *A Pilgrim at Tinker Creek*, Annie Dillard describes such an encounter with the gift:

> Last year I saw three migrating Canada geese flying low over the frozen duck pond where I stood. I heard a heart-stopping blast of speed before I saw them; I felt the flayed air slap at my face. They thundered across the pond, and back, again: I swear I have never seen such speed, such single-mindedness, such flailing of wings. They froze the duck pond as they flew; they rang the air; they disappeared. I think of this now . . . .
>
> It is the shock I remember. Not only does something come if you wait, but it pours over you like a waterfall, like a tidal wave. You wait in all naturalness without expectation or hope, emptied, translucent, and that which comes rocks and topples you; it will shear, loose, launch, winnow, grind. I have glutted on richness. . . . This distant silver November sky, these sere branches of trees, shed and bearing their pure

and secret colors—this is the real world, not the world gilded and pearled. I stand under wiped skies directly, naked, without intercessors. Frost winds have lofted my body's bones with all their restless sprints to an airborne raven's glide. I am buoyed by a calm and effortless longing . . . .

"It pours over you like a waterfall, like a tidal wave . . . that which comes rocks and tumbles you. . . . I have glutted on richness." That's a powerful description of the Life is a gift affirmation.

So, how do we make our way now from Dillard's experience to a Unitarian Universalist theology of giving? I noticed, by the way, that she was married in one of our Unitarian Universalist churches this past winter, and in *Pilgrim* she refers to a pet goldfish named Ellery Channing. So, maybe there is a way.

Persons who choose to affirm that life is a gift and who remain open to experiences that will bear that affirmation out also need ways to assure that the gift will always move. When a gift stops moving, it ceases to be a gift. This, according to Lewis Hyde, is what the Native Americans tried to teach the first European settlers on these shores. For their efforts, they were rewarded with the pejorative, if not racist, epithet, *Indian giver*. For the Englishman, the gift was to be kept, hoarded, and taken out of circulation in the hope that it might accrue even greater value in the future. But as Hyde points out, "The Indian giver understood a cardinal property of the gift: Whatever we have been given is supposed to be given away again, not kept. Or, if it is kept, something of similar value should move on in its stead. . . . In fact, it is better if the gift is not returned but is given instead to some new, third party."

There, my liberal religious friends, is the simple kernel for a theology of giving. *Life has been given to us by that which is greater than we know, and in order for it to remain a gift, it must remain on the move.* We move that life/gift personally by sharing it with those whom we love and care about, those to whom we choose to extend our lives. We have also created institutions, fallible and flawed institutions to be sure, but institutions nonetheless, the purpose of which is to nurture and enhance this life/gift, to carry its promises and possibilities from one generation to another. These are institutions that will, to paraphrase the Preamble to the U. S. Constitution, "secure the blessings of [life] for ourselves and our posterity." At their best, this is what religious institutions also do; they secure the blessings of life for ourselves and our posterity. At their best, this is what our Unitarian Universalist societies and our Unitarian Universalist Association do. We trip and we fail in our efforts at times. Religious institutions, after all, are only human. But we continue to believe that life is worth the effort, and that providing the place where and the means whereby this life/gift can be moved along is worth the effort.

So what does all this have to do with money? A great deal, as a matter of fact. As I dimly recall from a bonehead economics course, which was as far as I ever got with the subject, money is a symbolic means of characterizing and exchanging a certain portion of our life possessions. It is a tangible symbol of what we have, what we earn, or what we are fortunate enough, in some cases, to have been given. It is a concrete way of representing at least a part of the make-up of this life/gift. As such, our money offers us the means and the opportunity to keep the life/gift moving by supporting the institutions we have created to nurture and sustain that gift. Remember, "It is better if the gift is not returned but is given instead to some new, third party."

Institutions that attempt to secure the blessing of life are worthy third parties. Furthermore, our financial support also accords us the personal credibility we need to keep these institutions honest and focused on their task. It is our financial support of institutions that allows us to call them to responsibility and accountability when it comes to their making of our world a more human and humane place.

No, money can't buy the gift of love, it can't buy the gift of caring, it can't buy the gift of justice, and it can't buy the gift of peace. It can provide a setting, however, where if the proper human element is also present, love and caring and justice and peace can occur. Our Unitarian Universalist Association and our Unitarian Universalist churches, societies, and fellowships seek to offer such settings where these gifts are bestowed. Our financial support of our church and our Association is one of the means by which we can move the gift of life.

When persons looking for a place to freely pursue their spiritual journeys find a welcoming Unitarian Universalist congregation, the gift moves along. When we extend our support to those community organizations seeking to meet some vital human need, the gift moves along. When our Association helps to fund an extension ministry program for a small congregation seeking to grow, the gift moves along. When our Service Committee acts to redress an economic or political injustice, the gift moves along. When our Association's Office of Gay and Lesbian Concerns attempts to reduce the level of homophobia in our lives and our society, the gift moves along. When women and men in our seminaries struggle with what it means to be liberal religious ministers in the 1990s, the gift moves along. When the money we share makes all this happen, the gift moves along. And when it comes to the programs and outreach projects of our Association, what you just got was the very short list.

If we can affirm, then, that life is a gift, and if we can believe that life is, in some way, sacred, then our moving the gift along is a sacramental act. Filling out a pledge card in a generous fashion, or placing a contribution in a collection plate or box, or sending a check to our Association's Annual Program Fund may not seem like sacramental acts, but in the truest sense of the word, I believe they are. Among other things, a sacrament is a means of expressing gratitude and thanksgiving for the life we are given. To offer a *financial* portion of our life/gift in order to keep the gift moving is not something to be downplayed or hushed up then, but rather an act to be joyfully celebrated.

I'll close with some expressions of thanksgiving of my own. I thank Annie Dillard for her skillful way of capturing with words life's profound givenness. I thank Lewis Hyde for providing a marvelous account of what it means to be a giver of gifts. As one who also originally came to this country from England, I offer a very belated thanks, on behalf of my British ancestors, to those Native Americans who tried to teach them that the gift must always move.

∾

Personal Reflection

What do you consider to be the most important elements of the gift of life? How do you seek to keep the gift of life moving? How do you pass on the energy and blessedness that you have been given?

For the Congregation

1. Has a theology of giving been articulated in your congregation? Do you include it in your website or new member orientation? Do you pull it out each time you run a financial campaign? Does it guide the committees devoted to stewardship and development?

2. It would seem that the theology of "keeping the gift moving" applies to more than financial matters. Could it offer a theological basis for your religious education? Your social justice? Your worship? Your rites of passage?

3. Steve Edington writes, "No, money can't buy the gift of love, it can't buy the gift of caring, it can't buy the gift of justice, and it can't buy the gift of peace. It can provide a setting, however, where if the proper human element is also present, love and caring and justice and peace can occur." Is your congregation such a setting? If so, what makes it so? If not, what would help it become one?

BURNING THOSE BUSHELS

REV. JUDITH WALKER-RIGGS
All Souls Unitarian Church
Kansas City, Missouri

Sometimes Unitarian Universalists are shocked to be asked this question about their religion: "Is there a there, there?" As Judith Walker-Riggs suggests in this generous sermon, we shouldn't be surprised by how little others know about our beloved faith, since we keep almost everything about it hidden. She challenges us to let our light shine because "to be a Unitarian Universalist is to believe in growth."

Walker-Riggs points out two significant barriers to growth: "fear of growth" and a "rotten theology of money." She says we hide the fear of growth under a bushel of warm fellowship, claiming, "That's what's nice about being small." As to the rotten theology of money, she says, "We are suspicious of money. We do not rejoice at the large donor; we wonder what he's up to."

Building a culture of abundance requires being out in the open about money; it means burning the bushel of scarcity and shining with the power of generosity. As Walker-Riggs puts it, "The only thing I can remember the Old Testament saying you couldn't say was the name of God, Jehovah. Let's quit making money so much a God that we can't even say the name."

That's part of the "there" folks are asking about. —T. S.

163

Now Moses was keeping the flock of his father-in-law, Jethro, the priest of Midian; and he led his flock to the west side of the wilderness, and came to Horeb, the mountain of God.

And the angel of the Lord appeared to him in a flame of fire out of the midst of a bush; and he looked, and lo, the bush was burning, yet it was not consumed.

And Moses said, "I will turn aside and see this great sight, why the bush is not burnt?" When the Lord saw that he turned aside to see, God called to him out of the bush, "Moses, Moses." And he said, "Here am I."

—Exodus 3:1-4

IN THIS STORY, ancient Hebrews gave witness to the symbolic importance of flame and fire in religion. To this day, flame and fire are important in Judaism, in the menorah candles, in the candle lit at the beginning of worship every Friday night, in candles lit at home. Jews are not alone. Roman Catholics burn candles and incense, Chinese burn paper symbols at a funeral, the Zoroastrians make flame and fire a center of their very theology, and Unitarian Universalists, yes, even Unitarian Universalists, have the flaming chalice.

The association of the flaming chalice with liberal religion began in the late 1300s with Jan Hus, a Czech priest who offered the wine cup of communion, the chalice, to all people, not just to the priests, because he believed in the equality of all people under God. For this radical teaching, Jan Hus was burnt to death at the stake. The flame joined the chalice. And *that* flaming chalice was worn on cloaks as a secret emblem of religious liberalism almost six hundred years ago!

Just after the Second World War, the Unitarian Universalist Service Committee and the American Unitarian Association became serious about using the flaming chalice as *our* symbol of liberal religion too. It has come to mean even more than the equality of all peoples and the struggle for freedom of Jan Hus, as profound as these issues are. For us now, it means the fire of the human mind, the burning glory of life, the flame in the human soul, the light of reason—well, you fill in the blanks.

The chalice is growing in meaning, too, as in many Unitarian Universalist congregations across the country it is lit Sunday by Sunday, often by a different member of the congregation each week. I have heard a woman from a Jehovah's Witness background rejoice, with tears in her eyes, at the beautiful freedom she has found among us. I have seen a straight, sixty-year-old, usually three-piece-suited businessman light the chalice while dressed in a peach silk ball gown with rhinestone earrings hanging by his grey crew cut. (He was advertising a church dance, and in what other church but ours?) I heard a man dying of cancer celebrate the birth of his first grandchild that very morning at 3 a.m. I have seen thirty children parade into church, bent over under miles of crepe paper, dressed as one enormous Chinese dragon to light the chalice for the Chinese new year. I have seen a whole congregation weep as a mentally retarded boy lit the chalice, his first ever words in front of a group. The light in that chalice grows in meaning.

And I think back to my youth, for I am one of those rare birds, a born and bred Unitarian Universalist. I think back to our youth group conferences. (I am so old that I was in the AUY, American Unitarian Youth, before there even *was* an LRY, let alone a YRUU). I think back to our lighting of the chalice, followed by our raucous singing of "This Little Liberal Light of Mine." How we enjoyed clambering on the chairs in the "All around this world of ours" verse. And how we shouted as we sang, "Hide it under a bushel? *No*!!!"

If Moses had hidden his burning bush under a bushel basket, if Moses had never said anything about it to anybody, it wouldn't have attracted much attention, would it? He let that baby burn. And told them all about it.

And in the sincerity of my youth, that's what I *thought* we Unitarian Universalists were all about. Let that baby burn and tell them all about it. Hide it under a bushel? *No!!* Ah, but I have grown older now. And I have discovered that we UUs do seem to have a few bushels under which we tend to hide our light. I want to share with you what I think some of those bushels are and how we might burn them away and let the light shine.

Now the story goes that after Moses saw that burning bush, he led the children of Israel out of Egypt, where he had another vision, this time on a mountaintop. He came roaring down off that mountain with the Ten Commandments. And that's what I've got, my suggestions for a new set of Ten Commandments on how to burn those bushels under which we sometimes hide our light.

Why should we bother? Because people cannot be attracted to the light if it is not shining. The candle which remains unlit in the window guides no travelers home. Yes, I am talking about growth—growth in our congregations in numbers of people gathered, and growth in the power of what happens between those people once they have gathered.

I make no apologies for caring about growth. One of our Unitarian Universalist ministers, upon arriving at his new church, signed up himself, his wife, his son, and his mother, and when teased about it, said, "Hell, I'd sign up my *dog* if it was in the by-laws. I'm unrepentant about growth!" That church is growing. Now I might not go *that* far—I don't have a dog—but I, too, am unrepentant about growth. As a matter of fact, I agree with Tom Chulak that to be a Unitarian Universalist is to *believe in growth*.

We believe in growth in theology. We have grown through Reformation Europe, the Transcendental movement, and the beginnings of organized humanism, into process and feminist theology, and we aren't stopping now.

We believe in growth in ethics. We work for a better world with more love and justice, from Dorothea Dix fighting for the rights of the mentally ill to issues of racial justice and peace today. We believe in growth as an institution. We pride ourselves on being a changing movement, not a static denomination. We believe in growth sociologically. We wince at our white middle-classness and rejoice as Spanish and Korean congregations begin to celebrate our faith with large ethnic populations previously ignored. We believe in growth psychologically. Every year brings new adult courses created to help each of us with our own development. To be a Unitarian Universalist is to believe in growth. And I am very glad about that. It's why I'm here. But we do have a few bushels under which we hide our light. This is not an exhaustive list—exhausting maybe, but not exhaustive. It's just ten of the bushels I think we sometimes leave to cover our light, together with a new Ten Commandments to help us burn those bushels and set our light in the window to greet the world. They're not in any particular order, certainly not in order of importance. It was all I could do to come up with them, let alone arrange them artistically!

Bushel Number One: We have a tendency to bypass our modern history. If we think about our history at all, we refer to days long gone by. I say this as an historian—what's more, as the kind of historian whose idea of a lovely vacation is to spend months ploughing through ancient books by our forebears from 1500 to 1800, books whose dusty bindings activate my allergies. I get great joy out of relocating and reminding us of people long forgotten and the meaning of their stories.

I, of all people, respect our past, and want to help newcomers realize that we are not some just-struck match like Unification, but a flame that has been burning for centuries. But even I say unto you, we do hide our light when we ignore our modern history. Do you talk about Servetus and Channing? What about Emily Green Balch and Jane Adams, two of the first three women to win a Nobel Prize, both Unitarians? And the physicians' inter-

national peace group that won this year's Nobel Peace Prize? Two
of its five international directors are Unitarian Universalists. That
Nobel winning group grew out of the Physicians for Social
Responsibility, which held its first meetings at the Arlington
Street Church.

Then there was the recent Boy Scouts affair. You probably
read about it. There was a boy who could say his Boy Scout
pledge, including duty to God, as long as he was free to define
God. But he couldn't go along with the Boy Scouts manual, which
defined God *for* him as a "Supreme Being." You may also have
noticed later reports that the Boy Scouts changed their policy,
affirming duty to God but not defining it, and reinstated the scout
who began the debate, promoting him to life rank.

Do you know how it happened? While one long-time
Unitarian Universalist and ex-Boy Scout official was lobbying his
ex-colleagues on the Boy Scout Board, the new UUA president,
Bill Schulz, asked that he and executive vice president, Kay Montgomery, be invited to meet with the Boy Scout leadership. Bill
helped them consider the difficulties of defining God, even as a
supreme being, for after all, that just leads to having to define
supreme being. And the Boy Scouts' Board discovered that it was
not so easy to define God. Consequently, they resolved, "while not
intending to define what constitutes belief in God, the Boy Scouts
of America is proud to reaffirm the Scout Oath and its declaration
of 'Duty to God.'" That phrase, "while not intending to define
what constitutes belief in God" was wording suggested by UUA
president Bill Schulz.

I think we need to tell these stories to each other and to our
neighbors.

Bushel Burning Commandment One, then: *Thou shalt pay
attention to our modern history and spread the word.*

Bushel Number Two: We have a tendency to fear growth. The good
side of this is that we value the community we already have. Our

specialty, many Unitarian Universalists will say, is warm fellow-ship. (I'm sorry to tell you that there's really nothing special about saying that; what *would* be unusual would be to hear someone say, "What *I* like about our church is that it's so cold and unfriendly." We *all* think our churches are more or less friendly, at least to us, or we wouldn't be there!) But some of those who say that their specialty is warm fellowship then go on to say, "That's what's nice about being small."

I'm not so sure about *that*. Alice Blair-Wesley, a ministerial colleague who has spent years working primarily with small churches, has written, "Far more often than not, the small church, priding itself on its warm fellowship, is actually a stinging hive of old hurts, suspicion, backbiting, and vicious power struggles. That's *why* it's small. Warm fellowship, indeed!"

But E. M. Schumacher's book *Small Is Beautiful* seems to have gotten stuck in our mentality as some sort of creed even for our congregations. It reminds me of a cartoon I have on my wall. Two churches stand side by side. One is enormous, brick, Victorian, turreted, and towers over the other which is small, clapboard, single-steepled. Outside the second little church, there is a sign strangely like a Unitarian Universalist Wayside Pulpit, which reads in large letters, "Half as big and twice as righteous."

It may be that there is nothing particularly righteous about churches being either small or large. Powerful community *can* be found in larger congregations and is found there; that's why they are large. And if we want to bring our visions, our principles, and our faith powerfully to bear on the society around us, we may do better if we are not an exhausted dozen. I feel some sense of obligation to welcome the searching person who has finally made it to my church and hope that for them, as for me, that it may be a discovery of home.

Bushel Burning Commandment Number Two, then: *Thou shalt remember that a number is a person. To be interested in growing in numbers is not necessarily to sell out to mathematics. It may be just helping people as we have been helped.*

Bushel Number Three: We have a tendency to under support the Unitarian Universalist Association and its districts. The good side of this is that we are so proud of our local congregation that we really *do* believe that we have done it all ourselves.

A question frequently heard around budget time in a local church is, "Well, what have we ever gotten from them anyway?" I have heard this question asked by the Board of a Unitarian Universalist church even as they sat in a brand new building made possible by UUA and Veatch Committee grants—asked in front of the interim minister assigned and trained by the UUA, and the minister of religious education trained by the UUA and using UUA curricula, just after the most successful canvass ever, using UUA guidelines.

The next time that congregation met at a pot-luck dinner meeting, I did a very simple thing. I am going to do it with you now. I am going to ask you if you had ever heard of Unitarian Universalism before you entered the congregation that you now attend, would you please stand? If you had ever heard of Unitarian Universalism before you entered the church you now attend, would you please stand? I rest my case.

Bushel Burning Commandment Number Three, then: *Thou shalt not ignore thy denomination in times of need, for truly you have already reaped more from it than you have sown.*

Bushel Number Four: We have a tendency not to care for our property. Unitarian Universalist churches are often not the best kept in the neighborhood. Once, on a weekend visit to a distant church, I had a disturbing dream. I was up on a thirty-foot ladder at that church with a bucket and squeegee, cleaning its enormous and filthy windows. Alice Blair-Wesley hears people say, "It doesn't matter how the building looks. We come here for spiritual reasons. We're too busy to plant or clean or trim. And we can't afford to hire someone. We do get income by renting out our building during the week. Yes, that means sometimes we can't run a program of our own, and the utility bills go through the leaky roof, and renters leave the place dirty and unattractive, but how would we pay the bills without the rental income? Besides, we wouldn't want anyone to think we had an edifice complex. We serve the community by renting without proper accounting or custodial help. Yes, now that you mention it, the religious education rooms are filthy and unsightly. Why don't we have more children? Must be the birthrate has gone down."

Many Unitarian Universalists are rather well-to-do (very well-to-do in comparison to the population of the world, my friends) and live in fine homes. Why, then, is the church a mess? I sometimes wonder if we are trying to make up for, atone for, and break out of our comfortable suburban lives by recreating some simpler, less materialistic, and holier place in our messy churches.

In the Myers-Briggs Type Preference Indicator, which some of you know, in one category people score either as preferring to work from ideas down to details or as preferring to work from details up to ideas. Now, 75 percent of the general population of this country is in the second group, tending to prefer to work from facts, sense data, and details, up to, if they ever get there, the *big* ideas. Only 25 percent of the general population of this country prefers to work from the big ideas down to, if they ever get there, the little details. However, 95 percent or so of Unitarian Universalists score as big thinkers, even though such types are only 25 percent of the general population. That's not an excuse, folks. But it is an indication that perhaps we need to be more intentional about taking care of our details.

Do not be mistaken. It matters immensely how the church looks. It matters how the children's rooms look. When a newcomer arrives and everyone talks about the Brown room and the Channing Room, and there are no signs on the doors, let alone any map in a central place, they get the clear message, "We don't

want anybody who doesn't already know his or her way around."
When newcomers arrive and the yard is a weedy wreck and the
dust has settled on the hymnals, they will make assumptions
about how much this place really matters to its people.

Bushel Burning Commandment Four, then: *Thou shalt care
for the property of thy church, so that the shining light may reflect
through clean glass.*

Bushel Number Five: We have a tendency to be less flexible in our
organizations than we think we are. The good side of this is that
we are loyal. But inflexibility may make us slow to adapt to new
conditions. Once, at a ministers' meeting, Dana McLean Greeley
explained it this way: Other faiths, he said, have their creeds, their
central beliefs, at the hub of their institutions. If, for example,
their hub is, "Believe in Jesus Christ and you shall be saved," they
can try *anything* that might lead someone to that belief. They only
get nervous if someone says they want to change the belief. We, on
the other hand, Dana said, being less sure what that central *faith*
might be, have had a tendency to make the institution itself the
hub of our affairs. And we get plenty nervous when someone suggests we change the way *that* works. Indeed, some Unitarian
Universalist churches go from being the size of a family to being
a relatively large church without changing institutional systems.
People waft in and out of these churches' revolving doors as they
find that, friendly as people are, there is no meaningful way into
the real power structure of the church. Oh, they can be seized
upon to do some specific task and sucked dry, but they never really
got to the decision-making heart of the church. (I have another
cartoon on my wall. It's of a mountaintop, with a bearded guru
and a few children standing at the top, in the clouds. A bug-eyed,
torn, and bloody pilgrim is just fingernail pulling himself up the
last foot of the long, rocky mountain path. The guru says,
"Welcome, O weary searcher for truth! Say, have you ever worked
with kids?") Someone finally wends his way into your congrega-

tion because he seeks a spiritual home, some help defining values, some support in juggling the sixteen balls of his life, and we hand him another ball.

Aware of the stress most of us live under—our crazy schedules and calendars—many churches opt for one-person committees. Alice Blair-Wesley hears people say, "People are busy. Committee meetings are dull and uninteresting. Besides, a few key members of this church know, without discussion, what everyone else wants. Who needs meetings?"

She responds, "One-person committees are tyrannical, hidebound, and deadening, even if headed by a naive saint." Committee meetings, she says, "should be, can be, and must be—if the free church is to thrive—lively, creative, power-sharing, and profoundly religious occasions which summon novelty and personal growth regularly. Without effective and rotating committees, no church is free. On the contrary, the whole organization is trapped in a fierce lockup of stale ideas and procedures in mediocrity."

Having trouble staffing *your* committees? Are we lazy? Or do we just have a fine appreciation for life? Whatever, it is disheartening to find the people who are most suited to the leadership tasks you need done at your church are also the people most likely to have such a good sense of their own schedules that they know when to say no. Meanwhile, those who often are not much good at anything don't know how to stop themselves and go on volunteering for things at which they will be a disaster.

But is this the fault of the people, or the structure? Are some jobs too big? Do we see clearly the relationship of the committee job to be done with the overall mission of the congregation? There's an enormous change in the patterns of American family life, with working mothers, single families, increasing numbers of retired people. Chances are that means we've got to change our patterns. We need to plan ahead of our growth if we are to grow. To program only on the basis of actual growth is always to be at least one to two years behind the real momentum.

It's important, folks. Because what I see coming into our churches are people in a spiritual and ethical and faith search who are not looking for a free ride but who are looking for a place that will make demands on them for something that *matters*—a place that will help them make their lives mean more. Believe it or not, that place could even be a church committee.

Bushel Burning Commandment Five, then: *Thou shalt welcome not only new ideas but new ways of doing things.*

Bushel Number Six: We have a tendency toward rampant individualism, which we sometimes translate as my way, or not at all. (There have been dark days on which I have wondered if, somehow, Unitarian Universalism had become a religion for the socially inept, those who no other church would put *up* with!)

Obviously, individualism has a good side. For the Pope can say that the church is the final religious authority, and the Protestants can say that the Bible is, and the Hebrews can say that tradition is, but I am an unrepentant Unitarian Universalist who still believes that, in the final analysis, we all, each of us, are, as individuals, our own final religious authority. But we are such individualists, if we are Unitarian Universalists, in community. We are rampant individualists in a community of other rampant individualists. I sometimes hear people quote that old saw about how many people out there may be "Unitarian Universalists without knowing it."

There's no such thing, folks; there's no such thing as a Unitarian Universalist who doesn't know it. Oh, there are lots of people out there, no doubt, who share some ideas held by some Unitarian Universalists and who might enjoy knowing that a community of people like themselves exists. But this does not make them Unitarian Universalists without knowing it because to be a UU is not just to share certain beliefs, for indeed we have no creed. No, to be a UU is also to be involved in a community that defines itself as Unitarian Universalist. If you *are* a UU, you *know* it.

Such communities of rampant individualists have their problems. In the very first Unitarian church I ever served, the congregation was trying to decide between repairing the organ or buying a piano. I asked the treasurer what he thought. He replied, in his wonderful accent, "Ah 'aven't made oop mah mind yet, but when Ah do, Ah shall be very bitter." I have another cartoon on my wall, this one of an elderly couple lugging an enormous organ, pipes and all, out of a church. In the church doorway, one minister is saying to the other, "Yes, they donated it, but they didn't care for the prelude today."

Real relationship in community, on the other hand, accepts not only the possibility of changing others in our interactions with them, but equally, the possibility of being changed by those others. The French writer Stendhal said, "One can acquire everything in solitude, except character." Each of us individualists needs the community of other individuals to both challenge and support us.

Let me give you a glimpse of that in practice. During one Unitarian Universalist summer conference in the Pacific Northwest, the United States Navy was about to deliver a Trident nuclear submarine up the Hood Canal, on the anniversary day of Nagasaki, no less. Some of the conference participants were going to stand in silent vigil on the canal to protest the delivery of such a weapon, on such a day, to their neighborhood. Others believed that Trident subs and nuclear weapons are necessary, sadly necessary, but necessary. They approved of the delivery, and so they did not go stand in vigil. Yet many of them, nonetheless, gathered on the porch in the late afternoon of that long, rainy day to welcome those who held vigil home with hugs, hot chocolate, tears, and questions. "What happened?" "How was it for you, friend?" There was a community of rampant individuals where each felt free to act on what he believed, where each knew and honored the fact that what seems right to one seems wrong to the other, where people found ways to allow the love they bore for one another to transcend those differences in honor and hugs.

Bushel Burning Commandment Number Six, then: *Thou shalt honor other individuals as much as thyself.*

Bushel Number Seven: We have a tendency toward shyness. What?? Unitarian Universalists, shy?

Of course we are. The good side of this is that we respect other people and don't want to impose ourselves on them. But how long can it take us even to mention to someone that we *are* Unitarian Universalists, much less actually invite them to church? Yet statistics still show that nearly 80 percent of people start attending a church because of friends they know there. If you find a good book or movie, you may recommend it to a friend. Why not recommend a good congregation?

Bushel Burning Commandment Number Seven, then: *Thou shalt recommend a good church as quickly as you would a good movie or book!*

Bushel Number Eight: We have a rotten theology of money. This isn't just a tendency, folks; this is the big time.

The good side of this is that we aren't materialistic and don't make your welcome into our community dependent upon how much you can pay. But when Mary Kay Eliot was our UUA director of development and she was interviewing Unitarian Universalists of far more than average means for our capital fund drive, she constantly found ex-Unitarians. As one man said, he was tired of being given guilt trips over his Mercedes. We are suspicious of money. We do not rejoice at the large donor; we wonder what he's up to. The largest pledger in one church I know, annually pledging several thousand dollars more than anyone else, will take no position on a policy-setting committee or board of the church. At annual meetings, he sits at the back, where no one can see him vote, and never speaks. Why? He knows that if he does, others will think he's trying to push his weight around. What he gets for his money is disempowerment!

I was once at a church Canvass Kick-off Weekend where the Saturday evening dinner went great, but Sunday morning, the minister made a point of bragging in his sermon about how he wasn't mentioning money. The only thing I can remember the Old Testament saying you couldn't say was the name of God, Jehovah. Let's quit making money so much a God that we can't even say the name.

Bushel Burning Commandment Eight, then: *Thou shalt respect money for what it is, neither more nor less, and not be afraid to mention it.*

Bushel Number Nine: We have a tendency to be very slow to use new inventions. I *can't find* a good side to this one!

It's ironic. Our forebears *began* the Reformation by using that just invented, brand new machine, the printing press. We were among the first to see its potential to spread our words. Nowadays, we've got computers and VCRs. Or rather, the rest of the world's got computers and VCRs. Well, some of us have them in our homes. But in our churches? It somehow seems impure. Alice Blair-Wesley hears us saying, "We don't need quality office equipment. Our thirty-year-old mimeograph machine still works, doesn't it? If anyone needs copies, they can be made for ten cents apiece only eight blocks away, during business hours. Or one of our members can take the originals to work and bring them back next week, if he or she remembers."

Patterns of village communication will not work in the fast moving late twentieth century, where even rural areas are not villages anymore in the ways that they once were. There is nothing wrong with it just because it plugs in!

And what about television? There are increasing numbers of good Unitarian Universalist videotapes around. Univision, once a project of the Tulsa Unitarian Church, has become an independent corporation to produce Unitarian Universalist videos. Have you used its four-part history segment? Fusion is another video series from Rockford, Illinois. And how about the new UUA videotape with President Bill Schulz and Moderator Natalie Gulbrandsen?

There's going to be lots more happening. Be ready to pick up on it. In 1979, 69 percent of Americans had never heard of Unitarian Universalists. Only 4 percent had not heard of the Quakers, who are actually a smaller denomination. That's changing. In the next year, Bill Schulz will travel across the continent speaking on television and to the print media, a welcome change from the last few years of right-wing religious speakers. Bill will also represent the religious nongovernmental organizations at the celebration of the fortieth anniversary of the United Nations in December in Geneva, Switzerland.

Forrester Church is minister of All Souls Unitarian Church in New York. Next May, his book, entitled *The Devil and Dr. Church*, examining the guise of evil in modern life, will be published by Harper and Row, and it's a major publication for the period. The initial print run is set at fifty thousand copies. A companion book, *Wrestling with Angels*, is due for release in spring, 1987, and there is already some talk of boxed sets for Christmas 1987.

Will you have your local congregation mentioned on cable television by then? Maybe with regular shows from Univision? Univision will soon be an independent corporation, particularly to make video material for UU use. Will you be using it? And will you be ready for the strangers coming to your doors?

Bushel Burning Commandment Number Nine, then: *Thou shalt be a religion not only for the modern world but in the modern world. It's hard to convince people we're a modern religion if we use nineteenth-century techniques to spread our message.*

Bushel Number Ten: We have a tendency to believe that we are inarticulate in matters of our faith. The good side of this, I suppose, is that we don't go around hitting people over the head with our book. But *pish tush, pish tush,* I say we aren't inarticulate at all.

In fact, we've got a dandy set of Principles. Why don't you just repeat them after me:

The inherent worth and dignity of every person,

Justice, equity, and compassion in human relations,

Acceptance of one another and encouragement to spiritual growth in our congregations,

A free and responsible search for truth and meaning,

The rights of conscience and the use of the democratic process within our congregations and in society at large,

The goal of world community with peace, liberty, and justice for all,

Respect for the interdependent web of all existence of which we are a part.

Inarticulate indeed!!

Bushel Burning Commandment Number Ten, then: *Thou shalt learn the UUA Principles by heart. You heard me! By heart.* Why? Because, my friends, the world has need of them. In this world, where so many other messages sound out so loudly, our message needs to raise its voice too. In this world where a recent survey showed that 40 percent of Americans watch fundamentalist religious television for some measurable time every month, we need to speak up because this world has need of our vision; this world has need of our faith.

John Murray, the famous Universalist, said so long ago, "You may possess only a little light, but uncover it, let it shine, use it in order to bring more light and understanding to the hearts and minds of men and women. Give them, not Hell, but hope and courage!"

I'm going to ask you to join me now:

This little liberal light of mine

I'm gonna let it shine,
This little liberal light of mine
I'm gonna let it shine,
This little liberal light of mine
I'm gonna let it shine,
Let it shine, all the time, let it shine.

All around the neighborhood,
I'm gonna let it shine
[Repeat]

Hide it under a bushel, NO!
I'm gonna let it shine
   [Repeat]

We can do it, folks. Let's burn those bushels!

∽

Personal Reflection

Do you represent your faith in the wider world as often as you
would like to? If not, what prevents you from articulating your
faith or your beliefs to others?

For the Congregation

1. Judith Walker-Riggs' sermon was written in 1985. Given our
   experiences as Unitarian Universalists since then, are there
   any further commandments we might add to our tablet?
2. Walker-Riggs asserts that we can practice our beliefs only
   among other people. Tease out some of the things that being
   part of a congregation brings to your life that would be absent
   if you simply held to your beliefs in private.
3. Does your congregation ever hide its light under a barrel? In
   what ways? Why do you think this happens?

RELIGION THAT WORKS:
THE LAST HOW-TO SERMON

REV. GEORGE KIMMICH BEACH
Unitarian Universalist Church
Arlington, Virginia

Would that all Unitarian Universalists read and took Kim Beach's sermon to heart! If we all did, abundance of community, faith, and even money would be common in our congregations and our Association of Congregations.

Beach starts with this premise: "There is no help for the self (not even self-help!) which does not awaken to the fact that we are strangers to ourselves, lost in an inner cosmos until we give ourselves, our loyalty and devotion, to some life-enlarging cause . . . which calls us out of ourselves." Realizing this, he says "a fundamental turning point in our attitude toward religion," will come when we catch onto the fact that a religion that works *is one that goes to* work. *This is not the grandiose religion of earthshaking miracles, but rather the down-to-earth religion that makes our common acts of living meaningful and divine. A religion that works, that goes to work for ourselves and others, is about freely choosing to take full part, both financially and as an active participant in its meetings and celebrations, its committees and projects.*

Beach suggests that this "ordinary fact of religious commitment" carries over from individuals to our Unitarian Universalist Congregations freely joined in Association. Congregations should support their Association through the Annual Program Fund because "in many small, and a few large, ways, it has become our own." −T. S.

∼

THIS IS A HOW-TO sermon, as the title plainly indicates. "How to what?" you ask. Well, how to do whatever we most want and need to do. How to do the ordinary, desired, and needful things of human life. "How-to," *as such*. For present purposes, though, let's narrow the focus to what, I can only suppose, serves the same ends and concerns all of us here, the Unitarian Universalist religious enterprise. The how-to question then becomes this: How do we become a more successful, or a more effective, enterprise? Well, one or the other, if not both!

I've long been aware of the importance of how-to sermons, though I almost never give them. You know—"How to Deal with Religious Loneliness," "How to Live More Abundantly," "How to Do Well by Doing Good," "How to Be a Church Pillar Without Lending Visible Means of Support." That sort of sermon. If I could figure out *how to* preach such practical how-to sermons, maybe I'd be more effective, or more successful—well, one or the other, if not both. That's why I need a how-to of how-tos, as I suppose that, deep down, we all do. We need more than a few nifty suggestions on how to do this or that. Religiously, we are concerned with it all, with a last, an ultimate, even an eschatological *how-to*.

I first reflected seriously on this matter some fifteen years ago when I read the slogan on the signboard outside a Presbyterian church in downtown Cleveland. It said, "Religion That Works." Not a bad slogan, I thought. It's forthright, sensible, down to earth, practical. It promises results. If more people were more convinced that religion really worked for them, that it had a practical cash value, so to speak, then maybe more people would come to church. After all, people come to church, as they do anything, expecting some tangible return on their investment of time, energy, and money.

For several years, I often passed that church on my way to the old Unitarian church in the Hough district of the black ghetto, the area torn by riots in 1966. There, my colleague James Hobart and I pursued our urban ministry, called CUUP, the Cleveland Unitarian Universalist Parish. We worked with several inner-city grass roots organizations and sought to sustain support for them through the Unitarian Universalist congregations of the metropolis.

In short, we were attempting to generate a religion that works, though not quite in the sense that first comes to mind. We meant a religion that works not for ourselves but for others, whose lives were damaged by poverty, racism, welfareism, decayed housing and poor education—disintegrating communities struggling to be reborn. It was religion that works, all right, but without many success stories to tell for it. I wouldn't trade the experience of that work for anything.

Those events seem like ancient history to me now. The late 1960s, you may recall, was a time when the whole denomination went into a tailspin. Money, membership, religious education enrollment—everything declined. Nothing we'd been doing in the past seemed to be working very well any more. We yearned for some practical and personal how-tos. So after a decade of civil rights and other activisms, we began to withdraw into ourselves, into self, into spiritual and personal "growth." The 1970s became the age of the self-help therapies and the self-help books, *par excellence*. For instance, the book *How to Be Your Own Best Friend* pretty well sums up the concerns of a decade—reasonable concerns so long as you remember they're therapies, not theologies.

Given this trend, I suppose it had to come—a self-help book of self-help books, namely, Walker Percy's *Lost in the Cosmos: The Last Self-Help Book*. And there you have the true explanation of my title. I would have to give the preacherly counterpart to the

novelist's serious spoof. I'd have to give *The Last How-To Sermon*.
But let me give you Walker Percy's full title (most of it, anyway):

> *Lost in the Cosmos: The Last Self-Help Book, or, The Strange*
> *Case of the Self, Your Self, the Ghost Which Haunts the*
> *Cosmos, or, How You Can Survive in the Cosmos About Which*
> *You Know More and More While Knowing Less and Less*
> *About Yourself, This Despite 10,000 Self-Help Books, 100,000*
> *Psychotherapists, and 100 Million Fundamentalist Christians,*
> *or. . . .*
>
> *Why it is possible to learn more in ten minutes about the*
> *Crab Nebula in Taurus, which is 6,000 light-years away, than*
> *you presently know about yourself, even though you've been*
> *stuck with yourself all your life, or,*
>
> *How it is possible for the man who designed Voyager 19,*
> *which arrived at Titania, a satellite of Uranus, three seconds*
> *off schedule and a hundred yards off course after a flight of six*
> *years, to be one of the most screwed-up creatures in*
> *California—or the cosmos, plus,*
>
> *A Twenty-Question Quiz which will not help you become*
> *rich or more assertive or more creative or make love better but*
> *which may—though it probably won't, considering how use-*
> *less self-help books generally are—help you discover who you*
> *are not, and even—an outside chance—who you are, plus,*
>
> *A short history of the cosmos, including a semiotic theory*
> *of the self which explains why it is that man is the only alien*
> *creature, as far as we know, in the entire Cosmos . . . .*

There's a moral to this story. There is no help for the self (not
even self-help!) which does not awaken us to the fact that we are
strangers to ourselves, lost in an inner cosmos until we give ourselves, our loyalty and devotion, to some life-enlarging cause,
some greater good, some beauty of being that calls us out of ourselves. Hence, Walker Percy's is the last self-help book.

I asked myself, then, what would the sermonic analog be?

That there is no how-to of human being that does not finally leave behind the religion that works for me, or for us few (precious as I am, precious as we few are), to something vastly larger—to a religious new-mindedness that works for the life-enlarging cause, the greater or even the greatest good, the beauty and the joy of being that attracts us and draws us forth.

In other words, there comes a fundamental turning point in our attitude toward religion. This is the point at which we catch onto the fact that a religion that works is just one that goes to work. It enlists our talents and our energies, and yes, our financial resources to ends that fulfill our larger purposes, even our largest conceivable purposes as human beings.

I once heard Robert Frost say, "Education is a matter of hanging around until you catch on." I like that. And something like it, I imagine, could be said of our liberal religious community: Being a religious liberal is a matter of hanging around until you catch on, catch on to the fact that the only religion that works for me is the one that goes to work for others, for the human community, for the world. That is the life-enlarging cause that draws us together and sends us forth. That is the cause that attracts us and enlists our enthusiastic support.

It's odd that this should seem a great insight. It's the ordinary thing that motivates the very people who are the backbone of our congregations and our denomination, all the while we're trying to figure out *how to* bring in new folks with attractive but often skin-deep inducements, with clever slogans like "Religion That Works," or with clever sermon titles like "The Last How-To Sermon."

Perhaps you've heard it before. John Wolf, minister of the All Souls Church in Tulsa, said it first, "There is only one reason for joining a Unitarian Universalist church—to support it!" Meditate on that a while. John was saying something so straightforward, practical, and obvious that it seems, on first hearing, like a bold new insight. But it is the ordinary fact of religious commitment. It only seems extraordinary to the self "lost in the cosmos." It says, choosing to join a community of free faith means first of all that you choose to support it, financially, yes, but also participatively, as an active participant in its meetings and celebrations, its committees and projects. It means doing what James Luther Adams calls "the hum-drum work of a democracy."

Most of what goes on in our congregation, after all, is rather ordinary, unglamorous stuff, like un-trashing the grounds in what a *New Yorker* cartoonist calls "The Age of Trash." Maybe your congregation has a new-fangled idea every week. I don't know. But most of it at our place (Arlington, Virginia) is institutional maintenance with occasional innovations, with infrequent *peak experiences*, and with a genuinely heroic action every decade or so, like desegregating the northern Virginia parks in the late 1950s, or building a great new church sanctuary in the 1960s, or building Culpepper Garden retirement home in the 1970s, or becoming a sanctuary for Central Americans being hounded by our government in the 1980s.

But if you joined the church for these extraordinary things, then you may be a long time waiting. In the calmer reflections of the long run, you would realize that you joined it to help it be the kind of devoted, welcoming, labor-of-love community and the kind of self-governing and self-sustaining community that it most wants and needs to be. So valuing it, you support it. Your joining says, in effect, "We're here to stay, for the long haul."

If our congregation's annual canvass had been immediately ahead of us when I first gave this address, you might think that, under the cloak of a foxy sermon title, I was warming you up to giving money to the church. Not so! Our canvass was immediately behind us, an almost complete success. Rather, I'm warming us up to the idea of supporting the Unitarian Universalist Association, under the cloak of a foxy sermon title.

That is something you do not have to wait for your local annual canvass or any other extraordinary event to do. You can do it today by becoming a Friend of the UUA. A check of any size will do so long as it makes you feel good. Good grief! After fussing year after year over the right "Fair Share formula" for giving to our church, our canvass director, David Hunter, suggested this, not giving until it hurts but giving until it feels good. (I could call that "the last fair-share formula.") Giving, in other words, until you feel good about it because, after all, why did you join this church if not to support it? Or you can support the UUA by becoming a contributor to the $4 million capital-funding program called Visions for Growth, which President Eugene Pickett has initiated (and his successor will no doubt carry to completion).

Then, too, there's the ordinary year-in year-out way in which all of us support it, through what we appropriate directly from our church budget for the Annual Program Fund of the UUA. (Sure, but until it feels good?) This is our church's regular, and regularly fulfilled, way of lending support, so long, at least, as we don't clip away at it when the virtually inevitable budget-squeezing time comes—clip it and pare it out of first consideration for religion that works for us few and only secondarily works for the Unitarian Universalist movement itself. I hasten to add that our church is fulfilling its designated Fair Share to the UUA this year. But that's not extraordinary or especially commendable. To use Flannery O'Connor's fine phrase, it is merely our "habit of being."

So the truth is out. This is a sermon about denominational support. (An ill-kept secret in this hall, I dare say!) How we hate to talk about money! But as Ramona Barth of Alna, Maine, who used to live in Boston but now likes to call herself "Rural Ramona," said to Barbara Beach, "In the 1960s, sex came out of the closet; now you can talk about sex. In the 1970s, death came out of the closet; now you can talk about death. In the 1980s, money is coming out of the closet. Barbara, how much do you make?"

So, it's a sermon about money and denominational support! But what a stuffy, institutional word, *denominational*! Couldn't we call it a *movement*, as if it were going some place or doing something innovative? The word denomination calls up the image of a bureaucracy in far-off Boston, a host of Washington bureaucrats from my neck of the woods will say.

Had you been in our church the morning this sermon was originally given, I could have introduced you to a living, breathing Boston bureaucrat—Ellen Brandenburg, the current director for youth programs, and another, Wayne Arnason, Ellen's predecessor, who escaped to Charlottesville. They were doing the sort of thing such folks will at the grass roots, a training program on life issues for teenagers, LIFT for short. They seemed to enjoy it, as did those who gathered from up and down the East Coast for the workshop. This is not "Hey, wow!" news. But it does have everything to do with the week-in, week-out work of being a liberal religious community that makes room for teenagers by making room for their real-life issues. This is but one example of good things happening due to our denomination, our bureaucracy which art in Boston, our UUA—one example of religion that works when we work for it.

It also exemplifies an entirely ordinary, churchly concern, typical of any effective or successful religious community: to make room for the life issues of the younger generation, so as to confirm and sustain their participation in its ongoing life, so as to be a people who make room for each other by taking each other's life crises and life triumphs seriously. The UUA helps it happen and keep happening among us. Therefore, join the UUA. That is, support it!

You see, I have no surprises. Come to hear a good old how-to sermon, and what you get is some practical, how-to advice. Maybe it's a little more practical than you were counting on, to be told to participate, to be the kind of pillar that lends visible means of support. This is our normal, expected, ordinary way of joining the institution that is part movement, part denomination, and altogether our own.

Gifts do come back to us from headquarters, for instance, Charles Stephen's 1985 Meditation Manual, *The Gift of the*

Ordinary. His title derives from novelist Cynthia Ozick, in particular these words she wrote:

> The Extraordinary is easy. And the more extraordinary the Extraordinary is, the easier it is: "easy" in the sense that we can almost always recognize it. . . . The extraordinary does not let you shrug your shoulders and walk away.
>
> But the Ordinary is a much harder case. In the first place, by making itself so noticeable—it is around us all the time—the Ordinary has got itself in a bad fix with us: we hardly ever notice it. . . . When something doesn't insist on being noticed . . . we take for granted the very things that most deserve our gratitude.
>
> And this is the chief vein and deepest point concerning the Ordinary; that it does deserve our gratitude. The Ordinary lets us live out our humanity; it doesn't scare us, it doesn't excite us . . . . Ordinariness can be defined as breathing-space; the breathing-space between getting born and dying, perhaps, or else the breathing-space between rapture and rapture; or, more usually, the breathing-space between one disaster and the next. . . . In any case, the Ordinary is above all what is expected. And what is expected is not often thought of as a gift.

But it is. Mostly just by being themselves, the youth of our church have just recently been a gift to me. The Affirmation Class has become a regular, ordinary, every-other-year thing for our high schoolers. In this class, we deal with basic theological ideas, such as the meanings of God, of human being, and of religious community—ideas rooted in inescapable, human life-issues.

Following our class sessions this spring, several of us went to Boston, Cambridge, Concord, Salem, and Marblehead, in Massachusetts, to dig among the denominational roots, as well as for fun. I have seldom been back to the old town of Marblehead since leaving there for the Cleveland urban ministry in 1967. It looked pretty much as I remembered it and expected it to be, I'm glad to say. The old Town Hall, the narrow crooked streets, the antique house where we lived when our boys were very young, the ancient granite rocks by the harbor that, early on, somebody must have called "marble" (and it stuck), the church where I ministered, all so familiar and so mercifully unchanged.

It's like stepping back into one's former self—a place where one is now history, insofar as one is remembered at all—and sharing that with some young people to whom it is oddly new. It's not, really. It is old. It is but *a gift of the ordinary*, given away to some others, so that this history might enter into their being, in a movement ever so slowly spanning the generations.

For us, this trip was a first-of-its-kind experience; best of all, it will become expected, the usual thing, in years to come. How to do it? It takes a lot of advance work to arrange, but it works! You get out of it more than you put into it, but still, you do have to put something into it first—time, energy, money. The church is like that.

We support the movement and its sustaining institutions because in many small, and a few large, ways, it has become our own. It is religion that works because it has become part of our ordinary, everyday way of being Unitarian Universalists.

∽

Personal Reflection

Consider the work that you do for your religious community. When do you start to discern that religion working for you? How are the two experiences related?

For the Congregation

1. Kim Beach defines religion that works as "just one that goes to work. It enlists our talents and our energies, and yes, our

financial resources to ends that fulfill our larger purposes, even our largest conceivable purposes as human beings." How would your congregation define religion that works? Lay out the most important examples of religion working from your congregational history. What are the most important examples for you as individuals? Are the two lists different in any significant way?

2. Beach talks about "giving until it hurts" and "giving until it feels good," two phrases often heard in relation to fundraising in churches. What is the distinction between the two? Does that difference lie in amount of money or in attitude? Explain.

3. What are the most important ways your congregation could become a more successful, effective enterprise?

FURNACES AND FOOT WARMERS

REV. CHRISTOPHER GIST RAIBLE

First Unitarian Congregation
Toronto, Canada

Christopher Raible's tightly woven sermon is one of those worth revisiting every so often, or any time you might have forgotten the basic reasons we gather together, why we need an associational organization, and how our history informs everything we do. In language as clear as his understanding of our history, Raible draws the distinctions between early Unitarians and early Universalists, reminding us in the process why both histories must continue to inform how we regard ourselves and what we do in our communities.

Furthermore, the sermon provides a perfect introduction to the history and organization of Unitarian Universalism for any newcomer; it should probably be included in visitor or new member packets. Where else can you find so concise an accounting of both our individualism and our commitment to the common journey, of both our hesitation about institutions and our enthusiasm for them? Raible captures the tension and the conflict inherent in who we are.

That tension and that conflict inevitably affect conversations and feelings about raising money to support our churches. Raible's sermon offers a good starting point for any congregation's consideration of where it has been and where it is going. Ultimately, the sermon concerns the value and necessity of community in the religious endeavor, and thus it addresses the most essential consideration in fundraising.

This sermon is, quite simply, a classic. –S. M.

∼

AMONG THE ARTIFACTS of a church I once served was a small box, no bigger than the proverbial breadbox. It was made of perforated metal in a wood frame, and it had a handle to make it easy to carry. The box, I was informed by the church historian and archivist, had years ago belonged to a member who had brought it faithfully to church every Sunday in winter, full of hot coals. It was a foot warmer.

That member was not unique. Most members of the church in the late eighteenth and early nineteenth centuries brought foot warmers to church with them in cold weather. You see, churches in those days, in that part of the world, were not centrally heated; indeed, they were not heated at all. If one wanted to be warm in church, one had to bring one's own heat with one. Churches then were designed with fixed pews with doors on them to keep out the draughts. Once one was seated with one's family in one's own pew with the door closed, one could be quite cozy, especially if one had a foot warmer full of live coals to radiate its heat into the enclosed space. The heat of one's own family was kept close. If one were warm, one thought very little of the possible cold of others in their pews in some other part of the church.

Indeed, in those days, the pews themselves were owned or rented by families for their exclusive use. That was the way the church raised needed revenues—so much per year per pew, the rate varying with the location of the pew. One paid the annual assessment for one's pew, whether one used it or not.

That church was not in those earlier days (nor in my days either) free from controversy. One of the constant issues in that church—and in many a church in many a time—was the question of making it warm and keeping it warm.

Let me tell you of another church, the church in Rowe, Massachusetts. In the year 1787, the congregation called as its second minister the Reverend Preserved Smith. (Lovely name—his son was also named "Preserved" and so *had* also to become a minister!) Mr. Smith became pastor of the church and the town of Rowe (the two were the same in those days—there was only one church in town) and served faithfully, without significant controversy, for many years. Then, in the year 1821, Mr. Smith, as it were, came out of the closet. He declared himself publicly to be a Unitarian! Perhaps members of the congregation had already guessed as much; he'd been preaching there for thirty-four years.

Nevertheless, it could not have been easy for Mr. Smith to make his Unitarian principles so explicit. After all, it was only two years after Channing's famous "Baltimore Sermon," which proclaimed the basic ideals of Unitarian Christianity. The farther one lived from Boston, the more dangerous it was to claim the label Unitarian as a religious identity. In Boston, Channing was part of a group of ministers who shared similar ideas, but Mr. Smith had no such easily accessible support group. Rowe, in the western part of Massachusetts, was three days' travel from "the neighborhood of Boston."

Yet when the Reverend Preserved Smith made his public declaration, the congregation, apparently without exception, accepted his theology. There was no controversy, no division. The church became clearly Unitarian. Such acceptance of Unitarianism by the congregation also could not have been easy. In many a New England town, the *Unitarian Controversy*, as it later came to be called, divided churches. If a minister declared himself to be Unitarian and a majority of the members supported him, the minority would walk out. Across the street they would build another church, dedicated to "Trinitarian" Christianity. The Unitarian majority retained title to the church building, the land, the endowments, the communion silver. That was how many a

Unitarian church came into being, by taking over an existing church. (Our Universalist forebears, however, had to start from scratch and build their own churches.) If the Unitarians lost the vote, they might also withdraw and try to build a Unitarian church. Thus, many a New England town, to this day, has two church buildings glowering at each other. Until those early nineteenth-century controversies, denominations as we now know them were, in New England, virtually unknown.

But, as I have suggested, there was no apparent controversy in Rowe. The church did not split over theology. Two years later, however, there was a division, due not to theology, but to technology. You see, in Rowe it was proposed that the church install a stove to heat the building! It would no longer be necessary for members to bring their own foot warmers.

There is no evidence that Mr. Smith's preaching was less fiery after he came out of the closet. Nor did its newly accepted Unitarian identity make the congregation less hardy in withstanding draughts. I would like to think that when they became Unitarian, members began to think more communally and to be more concerned about warmth, but the records of Rowe show no such clear connection.

The proposal was adopted; the church installed a stove. But a number of members were so upset that they withdrew in outrage, moved down the street, and built another, unheated church! For neither the first nor the last time in history, a church divided, not over the centrality of theology but over the centrality of the heating system.

Does it really make any difference if a church has a furnace for all? Does it matter if it requires attendees who want warmth to bring their own foot warmers? In a church with a stove or furnace, one does not have to worry about bringing one's own heat to church. Warmth is a given. The place is comfortable on arrival. On the other hand, if a church does have central heating, one must from time to time worry about the heating system itself.

Who fuels the furnace? Who builds and tends the fires? If there is central heating, there must also be collective paying. Many a congregation has discovered that feeding a furnace is the most readily obvious reason for raising church finances.

Once a furnace is installed, its existence is never questioned again. The adequacy and efficiency of the furnace may often and long be debated, but the need is never again doubted. Individual foot warmers become quaint archaic artifacts to be put in glass cases to remind members of the strange ways of their religious ancestors.

I use this metaphor of foot warmers and furnaces to consider the collection of churches and fellowships which make up what is now called the Unitarian Universalist Association. Next year, 1985, it will be just two hundred years since the first gathering of churches called Universalist, since the first Universalist convention, as it were. Until that time, there had been individual Universalist churches here and there. In 1785, representatives from nine different congregations from three different New England states assembled in Oxford, Massachusetts, for the first convening (thus convention) of Universalists. Those gathered immediately agreed, although they thought of themselves as independent Christians, to accept the designation "Universalist." They were all preaching universal salvation, the doctrine that declared that all human beings are, in the eyes of God, worthy of saving. No loving God, they taught, would eternally damn anyone. Those old Universalists cared universally about the whole of humanity, thus distinguishing themselves from those around who taught that God only saved some and condemned most human beings to hell.

At that convention, they agreed not only to accept the identity Universalist; they agreed, also, that they all ought to be connected in one body, to quote them, "consequently bound by ties of love to assist each other at any and all times when occasion shall require." Let me repeat that last phrase. They promised to be "bound by ties of love to assist each other at any and all times when occasion shall require." That meant not merely within each church, but between churches. By 1785, the Universalists had already learned that individual congregations had need of each other. "Bound by ties of love," congregations had responsibility to and for each other. Congregations needed to warm each other. They were shifting from foot warmers to furnaces.

Next year, 1985, it will be just 160 years since the first formal association of Unitarians in North America. In 1825, in Boston, Massachusetts, the American Unitarian Association was organized. Let me quote, from the original statement, the reason those Unitarians constituted themselves. Their constitution declared that the "object of this Association shall be to diffuse the knowledge and promote the interests of pure Christianity." Again, "to diffuse the knowledge and promote the interests of pure Christianity." By pure Christianity, of course, they meant Unitarianism. By a curious coincidence, in the same year, 1825, in the same month, May, on the same day, the twenty-fifth, Unitarians in Great Britain were first organizing.

Please note: The Unitarians in Boston, unlike the Universalists in Oxford, were not joining for mutual assistance. They were associating to "diffuse . . . and promote" their religious ideals. They were, in a sense, concerned less with their own need of warmth and more with radiating out to the world.

That first Unitarian association, unlike the first Universalist convention, was not an association of congregations. It was an association of individuals! It took another half century, almost, for Unitarian churches to join together. The AUA, or American Unitarian Association, was an association of preachers and laymen (no women, alas, at first) who joined to "diffuse . . . and promote," that is, to publish. The main idea was to use the laymen's money to publish the preacher's sermons. That is essentially what happened, except that the Association could not be so limited.

The first report of the AUA the next year, 1826, outlined the activities of the year. The Association did more than publish. The report was filled with news of various Unitarian churches. It told of Unitarianism on the frontier west of the Allegheny Mountains. The Association helped finance a minister, thus the first extension minister, although he was not called that. Contributions were made to help construct a Unitarian church building in Pennsylvania. Auxiliary associations and regional groupings of Unitarians were being organized in various parts of the continent. To be in association meant much more than publishing. It meant to be involved in a variety of programs and activities (what we would today call *extension*) for knowledge to be diffused and promoted.

That first year, the new Association found that it had other problems. The treasurer's report revealed the receipt, as payment for some pamphlets, of three dollars in counterfeit money. Such were the trials of a budding bureaucracy!

The report indicated certain difficulties the Association had to face. There was resistance by some to the idea of joining together. Let me quote a few lines:

> The times require a more systematic union and a concentration of labors by which interest may be awakened and confidence inspired and efficiency produced. The want of union among . . . our denomination is felt to be a great evil by those who have directed their attentions to this subject. Living in an age of unusual religious excitement, surrounded by numerous sects, all of which are zealously employed in disseminating their peculiar tenets, we should be wanting in duty to ourselves and be doing injustice to the doctrines we profess, if we should allow them to fail in exercising their due influence for the want of a corresponding zeal and interest. Our exertions have not been apparent because insulated. . . ." [Note the word *insulated*, which means to keep one's heat in.] Or again we feel confident that there are among us men of zeal and energy who are both willing and able to exert themselves in the cause of religion and that

others who are now indifferent to the subject might by sympathy and encouragement be excited to similar exertions. All that is required is that they be brought together and acquainted with each other's views and feelings, that they be allowed to unite their labors in one common field and for one common end and thereby warm each other's hearts and strengthen each other's hands.

In seeking to unite to "warm each other's hearts," the American Unitarian Association was not a foot warmer; it was becoming a furnace.

Is our denomination a furnace? In a sense, yes. Through it, we collectively warm ourselves "by ties of love to assist." Its products and publications—books, pamphlets, periodicals, special reports, items dealing with religious education of children and adults, with worship, with program and administration—were all created to help us help each other. Our Association gives practical assistance in organization and fundraising through counseling and conferences. Our denomination helps provide leadership, especially ministers—their recruitment, training, settlement, unsettlement, assistance, retirement. But it also offers help to laypersons who are in leadership positions in congregations.

Our Association helps spread the news and the views of all of us who claim identity as Unitarian Universalists. Not a week passes when this—or, for that matter, any other Unitarian Universalist congregation—does not draw on the warmth of being a part of a larger association, though rarely do we think about that drawing, any more than we think about it when we turn up a thermostat or turn on a light.

Here in Canada, there is the Canadian Unitarian Council; across the continent there are districts or other geographic clusterings. These are but smaller geographic examples of the same associative feeling which originally created the furnaces of our Universalist and Unitarian continental organizations. These all exist so that we, the constituent members, may collectively warm ourselves better by assisting each other.

We associate also to "diffuse and promote," that is, to warm others. We have never been very effective missionaries. We do not want to convert other people. But we do reach out; we seek to extend our faith. Our own congregation here would not survive and thrive today without extension efforts by various denominational bodies at various times in our history. No Unitarian Universalist congregation on this continent would have been created, or at least long sustained, without our denominational association, without its programs to diffuse and promote, and thus help.

Our association's warming of others is not merely a warming of our fellow Unitarian Universalists across the continent. We warm others when we respond to social injustice in the world. Every movement for social reform in North American history had and has Unitarians and Universalists in significant leadership positions. In local communities at crucial times, our congregations have made a difference, as for example during the American civil rights struggles in the 1950s and 1960s. We may sometimes laugh at our Unitarian Universalist penchant for thinking that resolutions can bring revolutions, but our combined efforts have had profound effects on concerns like disarmament, public education, women's rights, and civil liberties. Every significant social issue of our time involves our stimulation, influence, and support through denominational associative activities. We work to spread our warmth, if not in theology, then in morality.

As a furnace, the Association heats all, and helps all of us and others too. When, two hundred years ago, the change of moving from individual foot warmers to collective furnaces began, something very special happened. When a congregation first installed a stove to heat everyone, it never put the stove inside, up front. A study of old churches reveals that a stove was always at the back of the church. The stove pipe went up, forward along the length of the room, and then up and out. The heat radiated from the pipe so that all were warmed, but the furnace was never the focus. It was never the center of attention. It was at the back, where it could be fueled and tended without distracting. Later, even better, furnaces were located out of sight in basements or boiler rooms. The ideal furnace warms a church and is never seen. The people are almost unaware of it. It is not thought about except when it does not work to warm.

Our feelings about furnaces, however, are reflected in a current advertisement for converting heating systems. The old furnace is portrayed as a monster—greedy, noisy, expensive, and overwhelming. We sometimes seem to fear that our denomination is such a furnace; that which unifies us may also dominate us.

The only purpose for our furnace is to warm our space. It is still up to us to provide whatever happens within the space. Further, in regard to our furnace, new leaders of our congregation go through a kind of initiation. Those elected to our board or property committee must be taught the intricacies of the heating system. Our best kept secret is how our furnace works. Our most sacred space, it seems, is our furnace room. Is there, perhaps, not also a similar set of feelings about our denomination and how it works?

Yet every one of us knows how important our furnace is. We all know that we must put money in if we are to get heat out. Every congregation I have ever known, unless it had a brand new heating system, worried about the boiler. When was the boiler going to blow up? In each of two churches I served, it did! Only boilers do not blow; they crack, leak, and lose pressure. They die more with a whimper than a bang. Denominational programs never blow up either; they merely crack, fizzle, and lose force unless they are properly maintained.

Central heating in churches brought another change. It broke down isolation. When stoves were put in, pew doors could be taken off. Even pews were no longer necessary once the whole place was heated. Central heating gave opportunity for flexibility and thus community. Heating was in common.

Our denomination is something like a furnace. Most of the time, we are unaware of it. Always is it important. Never is it central to our purpose. It exists to serve us; it is ours. We created it; we maintain it.

Have you ever noticed that ministers in church buildings always go around turning down thermostats and turning out lights? Ministers know that congregations always find money to pay the utility bills. The heat and the light are always paid for. Ministers turn down and turn off to lower utility costs so that there may be some money left to pay the other expenses. In all my experience (I grew up in the church), I have heard of congregations that stopped salaries, that cut programs, that delayed maintenance, that put off purchases. But I have never known of a congregation that did not pay the utility bills. Heat and light are always paid for.

Could we not also see our denomination in the same way? We must pay for it in full so that it will always be there for us to use when we want and need it. Not to support the Association is as irresponsible as not paying the electric bill. It is as simple and as ordinary as that. We should look for ways to improve its quality and efficiency, but we have no choice but to pay for it. Supporting our Association is not giving to a charity; it is paying for a utility.

But we should know that warmth, although important, is never enough. A few years ago, our denomination had an extensive extension program called Sharing in Growth. The program was based on four principles, summarized in four words: *warmth*, *breadth*, *depth*, and *growth*. *Warmth* meant the quality of the community that is a Unitarian Universalist congregation. *Breadth* meant the diversity of its activity and the variety of its programming. *Depth* meant its religious or spiritual concern. Growth referred to its openness to others, its eagerness to bring others into the circle of its community. Those involved in the Sharing in Growth program discovered that the first quality, warmth, was the easiest for members to get interested in, the most fun to work on.

A foot warmer mentality concerns itself only with its own warm space, while a furnace mentality worries about a larger environment. But to think simply of warmth is to forget what goes on within the space. Warmth itself is meaningless. It is essential, but there must be more.

Those who brought their foot warmers to church could, of course, have stayed home; it is warm at one's own hearth. If warmth is all one wants, one might as well stay home. Two hundred years ago, people came to church carrying their foot warmers because they wanted in their lives something more than they could get individually at home. They wanted and needed some connection with a community of persons and some connection with divine inspiration. That human and divine connection is what the church is always all about. Individually and collectively, we need that connection. Our name Unitarian reminds us that we seek to unite. Our name Universalist reminds us that we seek to be complete. Never need we be isolated; never need we be insulated. By connecting with each other and connecting with the divine, we feel a deeper and very special kind of warmth. Its radiation can change our lives and can transform our world.

∼

Personal Reflection

Christopher Raible's sermon suggests that as long as we have a religious community, we need never be alone: "By connecting with each other and connecting with the divine, we feel a deeper and very special kind of warmth." How has your community allowed you to experience that warmth?

For the Congregation

1. Christopher Raible shows that the privileges and luxuries of

community come with responsibilities. Can you think of times when your congregation wants the former without accepting the latter? How can you tie the two together in people's understanding?

2. Raible reminds us that early Universalist churches agreed to be "bound by ties of love to assist each other at any and all times when occasion shall require." Does your congregation have relationships with other congregations that fulfill this early covenant? Do financial resources play into the equation?

3. Raible suggests that for all Unitarian Universalists, institutionally speaking, the core furnace is the Unitarian Universalist Association. What is your congregation's core furnace, spiritually and theologically speaking? Does your congregation seek, like early Unitarians, to fund the fueling of that fire?

For Further Reading

Alexander, Scott W. *Salted with Fire: Unitarian Universalist Strategies for Sharing Faith and Growing Congregations.* Boston: Skinner House Books, 1994.

Barna, George. *How to Increase Giving in Your Church: A Practical Guide to the Sensitive Task of Raising Money for Your Church or Ministry.* Ventura, CA: Regal Books, 1997.

Block, Peter. *Stewardship: Choosing Service Over Self-Interest.* San Francisco: Berrett-Koehler Publishers, 1996.

Callahan, Kennon L. *Giving and Stewardship in an Effective Church: A Guide for Every Member.* San Francisco: HarperSan-Francisco, 1992.

Dunham, Laura. *Graceful Living: Your Faith, Values, and Money in Changing Times.* New York: RCA Distribution, 2002.

Durall, Michael. *Beyond the Collection Plate.* Nashville: Abingdon Press, 2003.

————. *Creating Congregations of Generous People.* Bethesda, MD: Alban Institute, 1999.

Green, William. *Inspiring Generosity.* Cleveland: Local Church Ministries, United Church of Christ, 2002.

Grimm, Eugene. *Generous People: How to Encourage Vital Stewardship.* Nashville: Abingdon Press, 1992.

Hoge, Dean R., Patrick McNamara, and Charles Zech. *Plain Talk about Churches and Money*. Bethesda, MD: Alban Institute, 1997.

Jeavons, Thomas H., and Rebekah Burch Basinger. *Growing Givers' Hearts: Treating Fundraising as Ministry*. San Francisco: Jossey-Bass, 2000.

King, Jerry. *Asking Makes a Difference*. Self-published, 2000.

Lynn, Robert Wood. *Understanding Religious Giving Styles*. Bethesda, MD: Alban Institute, 1999.

Ronsvalle, John and Sylvia. *Behind the Stained Glass Windows: Money Dynamics in the Church*. Grand Rapids, MI: Baker Books, 1996.

Scheyer, Fia B., Ruth Lewellen-Dix. *Stewardship: The Joy of Giving*. Boston: Unitarian Universalist Association of Congregations, 2000. **www.uua.org/re/curriculum/stewardguide**.

Shore, William H. *The Cathedral Within: Transforming Your Life by Giving Something Back*. New York: Random House, 2001.

Trumbauer, Jean M. *Created and Called: Discovering Our Gifts for Abundant Living*. Minneapolis: Augsburg Fortress Press, 1998.

Twist, Lynne. *The Soul of Money: Transforming Your Relationship with Money and Life*. New York: W. W. Norton and Co., 2003.

ABOUT THE
STEWARDSHIP SERMON AWARD

This award was established in 1984 by the UUA Development Department/Annual Program Fund (APF) and is now jointly sponsored by APF, the Unitarian Universalist Ministers Association, and the Liberal Religious Educators Association. It is presented annually for the sermon judged most effective in exploring and promoting financial support of Unitarian Universalism and in directly addressing money as it relates to affirming our Unitarian Universalist faith, vision, and future. The sermon must have been delivered before a Unitarian Universalist congregation within the previous fourteen months. There is a $1,000 cash award for the sermon, which is delivered at General Assembly during a worship service and made available in hardcopy and on the UUA website at **www.uua.org/giving/apf/sermon.html**.

2006 - Cecelia Kingman Miller
2005 - Naomi King
2004 - Bonnie McClish Dlott
2003 - Patrick T. O'Neill
2002 - Gary Blaine
2001 - Victoria Safford
2000 - Gary Kowalski
1999 - David R. Weissbard
1998 - Amanda Aikman
1997 - Virginia P. Knowles

1996 - Victoria Safford
1995 - Webster Kitchell Howell and David A. Domina
1994 - Keith Kron
1993 - Gary E. Smith
1992 - No award
1991 - Gary E. Smith
1990 - No award
1989 - Stephen D. Edington
1988 - No award
1987 - José A. Ballester
1986 - Judith Walker-Riggs
1985 - George K. Beach
1984 - Christopher Gist Raible

About the Stewardship Sermon Award Winners

Rev. Amanda L. Aikman serves Northlake Unitarian Universalist Church in Kirkland, Washington. She is a playwright and the creative director of BLUUBIRD Theater Company, a Unitarian Universalist drama ministry.

Rev. George Kimmich Beach edited three volumes of essays and addresses by James Luther Adams and authored *Questions for the Religious Journey* and *Transforming Liberalism: The Theology of James Luther Adams*. He has served Unitarian Universalist congregations in Massachusetts, Texas, and Virginia, and an urban ministry in Ohio. Rev. Beach is now retired from full-time ministry. He and his wife, Barbara Kres Beach, live in Falls Church, Virginia, and in rural Madison County, Virginia, where he writes, grows grapes, and makes pottery.

Rev. Gary Blaine is the senior minister of the First Unitarian Church of Toledo, Ohio. Gary writes and lectures on issues such as economic and racial justice. He is vice president of Planned Parenthood of Northeast Ohio, spokesman for the Citizen's Clean Campaign, and a member of the Rescue Mental Health Board.

Rev. Bonnie McClish Dlott lives in the San Francisco Bay Area with her husband, children, and cat. She is a graduate of Starr King School for the Ministry, currently serving the Unitarian Universalist Fellowship of North Bay in Napa, California.

DAVID A. DOMINA, a native Nebraskan, is one of the country's most seasoned trial lawyers. Domina has spoken to juries in half the states in the Union. Spiritual ideas are often part of Domina's professional work.

REV. STEPHEN EDINGTON has served as the minister of the Unitarian Universalist Church of Nashua, New Hampshire, since 1988. He has also served congregations in Stony Brook, New York, and Rockland, Maine. Steve is a co-author of *100 Questions Non-Members Ask About Unitarian Universalism*. He is also the author of *Kerouac's Nashua Connection* and *The Beat Face of God: The Beat Generation Writers as Spirit Guides*.

REV. WEBSTER KITCHELL HOWELL served Unitarian Universalist congregations in Arlington, Texas; Providence, Rhode Island; Ft. Lauderdale, Florida; and Lancaster, Pennsylvania. He died in 1997. His congregations knew and loved him for the charismatic speaker, caring minister, outspoken activist, and storyteller extraordinaire that he was.

REV. NAOMI KING serves the Unitarian Universalist Church of Utica, New York. She enjoys the ministry of stewardship and abundance.

REV. GARY KOWALSKI is the author of *Revolutionary Spirits: The Religious Beliefs of America's Founders* and best-selling titles including *The Souls of Animals, Goodbye Friend: Healing Wisdom for Anyone Who Has Ever Lost a Pet, The Bible According to Noah: Theology As If Animals Mattered*, and *Science and the Search for God*. He currently serves as minister to the First Unitarian Universalist Society of Burlington, Vermont.

REV. KEITH KRON is the director of the UUA Office of Bisexual, Gay, Lesbian, and Transgender Concerns. He revised the UUA *Welcoming Congregation* manual and wrote a premarital counseling guide for same-sex couples. He has worked for the UUA since

1996 and has traveled to more than four hundred congregations to preach and lead trainings.

CECELIA KINGMAN MILLER has been a stewardship consultant since 1999, working with individual congregations and leading workshops and trainings. She currently serves Wy'east Unitarian Universalist Congregation in Portland, Oregon, as a special consultant for growth. She is also vice president for development of Project Harvest Hope, a nonprofit organization providing sustainable development assistance to the Unitarians of Transylvania.

REV. PATRICK T. O'NEILL was ordained to the parish ministry in 1979. He has served UU congregations in Massachusetts and Delaware, and is currently serving as interim minister at the UU Fellowship of West Chester, Pennsylvania.

REV. CHRISTOPHER RAIBLE has served the Unitarian Church of Jamestown, New York; Unitarian Church West, Brookfield, Wisconsin; the First Unitarian Church of Worcester, Massachusetts; and the First Unitarian Congregation of Toronto, Ontario. All were "honor societies" during his years with them. He also headed two UUA departments, Communications and Extension. Having visited more than five hundred (addressing some two hundred) Unitarian Universalist congregations in North America and Europe, he lives in contented retirement in Creemore, Ontario.

REV. VICTORIA SAFFORD has been minister of White Bear Unitarian Universalist Church in Mahtomedi, Minnesota, since 1999 and is the author of *Walking Toward Morning*. She lives with her partner Ross and their twelve-year-old daughter Hope.

REV. GARY E. SMITH has been senior minister at First Parish in Concord, Massachusetts, since 1988. First Parish exceeded their pledge goal by $11 thousand in 1993 when Gary was on sabbatical. He was asked to leave on sabbatical again the following year.

REV. JUDITH WALKER-RIGGS is a life-long Unitarian Universalist who trained for the ministry at Oxford, England, and ministered for forty-one years with Unitarian Universalist congregations in Europe and the United States. From teen-aged service as an officer of Liberal Religious Youth to adult service on the Ministerial Fellowship Committee, the UUA Board of Trustees, and the Unitarian General Assembly Council in Britain, she has long believed in the necessity of strong relationships not only between Unitarian Universalist individuals but between congregations.

REV. DAVE WEISSBARD retires in June 2006 after twenty-seven years as senior minister of the Unitarian Universalist Church in Rockford, Illinois. He previously served the First Parish in Bedford, Massachusetts, and the Fairfax Unitarian Church in Oakton, Virginia.